ST. MARGARET MARY
Apostle of the Sacred Heart

St. Margaret Mary
APOSTLE OF THE SACRED HEART

by Ruth Fox Hume

illustrated by JOHANNES TROYER

Farrar, Straus & Cudahy
Burns & Oates

VISION BOOKS
New York
London

VISION BOOKS
IS A DIVISION OF
FARRAR, STRAUS & CUDAHY, INC.
PUBLISHED SIMULTANEOUSLY IN CANADA BY
AMBASSADOR BOOKS, LTD., TORONTO.
MANUFACTURED IN THE U.S.A.

For Ann

CONTENTS

AUTHOR'S NOTE

Paray-le-Monial is a small peaceful town 214 miles from Paris. If you leave the city on the morning Moulins Express you can be in Paray by early afternoon. I made the trip on the first Friday of July, 1957, the height of the French tourist season. In the Gare de Lyons I had seen pilgrims by the trainload setting off on the arduous overnight trip to Lourdes. But Paray, I found, was not the least affected by that summer's record influx of visitors. Its three hotels were offering a choice of rooms. There were about seven of us foreigners in town on that particular weekend: three Americans, two Swedes, and a few German students.

Paray has yet to be "discovered" by tourists and pilgrims in the sense that Lourdes and Lisieux and Fatima have been. Yet the thing that happened there is one of the most tremendous that ever happened in the history of the Church, and the saint who lived there three hundred years ago is one of the most glorious in the whole calendar of the Blessed.

In one way it is entirely in character that relatively few people go to visit the earthly home of St. Margaret Mary Alacoque. She herself felt very strongly on the subject. It was her greatest wish that after her death the Sacred Heart of Jesus, Whose disciple she was, would be honored by the entire world—and that she herself would be forgotten.

The first half of her wish has been abundantly granted. In his encyclical on the Sacred Heart, written in 1956, the late Pope Pius XII wrote: "Therefore, devotion to the Most Sacred Heart is so important that it may be considered, so far as practice is concerned, the perfect profession of the Christian religion." St. Margaret Mary's mission in life has quite clearly been fulfilled.

The second half of her wish, fortunately, has not been granted. But it is a safe enough guess that there are many people who go to Mass faithfully on every first Friday, who celebrate the great feast of the Sacred Heart, and who honor Its image in their homes without ever knowing how and when these practices began.

The story of Margaret Mary Alacoque, canonized in the year 1920, is also the story of another great soul, even less known than she. His name is

Blessed Claude de la Colombière and he is one of the glories of the Society of Jesus. He too rests in Paray-le-Monial, a few blocks away from the chapel where Christ revealed His flaming Heart to the humble Visitation nun.

The principal source of this book is the three-volume *Vie et Oeuvres de Sainte Marguerite-Marie Alacoque*, 1920 edition, edited by Monsignor Gauthey. These books contain the saint's autobiography and letters, the contemporary account of her life, the statements and affidavits of the people who knew her, and a wealth of material concerning the Visitation of Paray and the fascinating people who lived there three centuries ago. I would like to thank the Sisters of the Georgetown Visitation Convent in Washington, D.C., for their kindness in making available to me the three volumes without which no biography of the saint is possible.

Other sources of material were the modern biography of the saint published by the Visitation of Paray-le-Monial and the *Bienheureux Père Claude de la Colombière* by P. Louis Perroy. Books in English that proved most valuable were *The Sacred Heart in the Life of the Church* by Margaret Williams, R.S.C.J., and *These Three Hearts* by Margaret Yeo.

Finally I would like to renew my thanks—

although it seems a most inadequate word—to Mrs. Justine B. Ward and to Mr. and Mrs. Gregory Smith, whose vast generosity made it possible for me to pay the saint an unexpected visit in her own home.

ONE • JOY INTO SORROW

The Alacoques, like all good parents, loved all of their children equally. But like most parents, they could not help having a slight weakness for one of them: Margaret, their only daughter. Everyone, even her three older brothers, made a pet of the bright-eyed little girl.

For older brothers to admire a little sister speaks very well for the little sister. Margaret was a natural-born tomboy. She could ride and fish and walk fences just as well as Jean and Claude and Chrysostome. Together the four children would roam through the wild woods that surrounded their home, and make up wonderful stories and games about knights and dragons.

The Alacoques were the happiest, most affectionate family imaginable. Monsieur Claude Alacoque, Margaret's father, was a lawyer and notary. He was a gentle, soft-spoken man, a little *too* gentle sometimes in the matter of collecting his fees. But the family was comfortably well off. Their estate at L'Hautecour—the rambling old buildings and farm lands called "Les Janots"— was one of the finest in the parish of Verosvres. It was in this small Burgundian town, some two hundred miles south of Paris, that Margaret Alacoque was born on July 22, 1647.

When the new baby arrived, Madame Fautrières, the great lady of the near-by castle of Corcheval, offered to be her godmother. This was a great honor. It showed how deeply respected Claude Alacoque and his lovely wife, Philiberte, were among their neighbors. As the little girl grew older, her noble godmother grew to love her as though she were her own daughter.

When Margaret was four years old Madame Fautrières urged her parents to let the child come to the castle of Corcheval for a long visit. "Madame Alacoque is not strong," the lady said persuasively. "She has the new little Jacques to care for, and those great noisy boys to wear her out! Come, dear friends, do this favor for a lonely woman. Share your treasure!" What Madame did *not* add was that she wanted to get Margaret away, for a little while, from the very unpleasant neighbors who lived in the farm building adjoining the Alacoques' comfortable house.

These dreadful people, alas, were Monsieur Alacoque's relatives, so that Madame could not complain *too* much about them, crude and coarse as they were. She wondered how such a fine man could have come from such a family. "I hope that woman never has anything to do with bringing up my little Margaret," she thought one day, as she heard shrill-voiced Grandmother Alacoque screaming at one of the farm hands.

So Margaret, scrubbed and polished within an inch of her life, was duly delivered to the chateau of Corcheval by her proud father. "It is good to have a little girl in this house again!" Madame Fautrières said to Margaret, when she had the child to herself. "*So* good! My own little girls are far away from me!"

"Oh, Godmother!" said Margaret, full of sympathy. "That is too bad. Where are they?"

"One of them is married to a great lord and

lives in Paris, at the court of the king. The other one is a nun."

Margaret's eyes widened. She knew practically nothing about nuns, but the thought appealed to her. "A nun? Where does she live? What does she do?"

Madame Fautrières smiled at the rapid line of questioning. "At the Visitation convent in a little town not far from here, called Paray-le-Monial. What does she do? Why—she prays."

"How happy she must be!" the little girl said.

Madame Fautrières stood up. "Come, *ma petite*, let me take you to your room." The child's naïve words had cast a shadow over her heart. She *hoped* that her daughter was happy, but the girl had not really had a vocation. The unholy custom of sending a second daughter off to the convent, if dowry money ran short, was still in full fashion.

Every year after that Margaret went to her godmother's home. The long visits at Corcheval were happy, but a little lonely. There were no children of her own age to play with. Madame, after the first novelty of the visit wore off, left her more and more in the care of servants. But she was such an easy child to take care of that the maids assigned to this task took advantage of her goodness and left her to her own devices much more than Madame suspected.

Margaret was perfectly delighted with this arrangement. The chateau was surrounded by wooded groves and by long shaded alleys of yew. She loved to walk there by herself. But above everything else at Corcheval, she loved the chapel. At home the parish church was over a mile away. Only the great castles had their own chapels attached. From the time Margaret was four years old it seemed to her a wonderful and exciting thing to live so close to God. She spent hours in this chapel of Corcheval, kneeling on the cold stone floor, looking at the tabernacle and thinking her own thoughts.

One day when she was alone, as usual, in the chapel, a strange thing happened. Without really knowing what she meant or where she had found the words, Margaret said firmly, "Oh my God, I consecrate to you my purity, and I make you a vow that I shall never marry!" This was the first glimmering of her future vocation.

When Margaret was eight years old, Madame Fautrières married again and moved away from Corcheval. Margaret missed her godmother but she was secretly pleased that her long visits away from home were over. So was little Jacques, her baby brother. He was now old enough to realize that big sisters pay much more attention to little boys than big brothers do.

Margaret loved to read to him. Books were scarce and expensive in those days, but Monsieur Alacoque, to the amusement of his crude relatives, bought all he could afford. Margaret's favorite book was a well-worn *Lives of the Saints*.

"Come Jacques," she told her brother one day, opening the book. "I'll read to you. Where shall we start?"

"Oh, let's read St. Sebastian or St. Laurence. I *like* them!" said Jacques, slightly bloodthirsty, like most small boys. "Or how about St. Genevieve? She was *brave*!"

But Margaret was leafing through the book thoughtfully, paying no attention to him.

"What are you looking for?" he asked her after a while.

"I'm trying to find a saint who's easy to imitate!" said Margaret.

In 1655 the sweet life that Margaret had known came to an end. It ended completely and abruptly, like the smashing of a delicate crystal. Monsieur Alacoque died suddenly. He left his wife and children provided with very little cash in hand. Optimistic and generous all his life, it had never seemed important to him to put his affairs in order. Poor Madame Alacoque, whom he had treated as tenderly as a child, had never given a thought to how the family business was run. Her husband's account books were a dark mystery to her. But as she pored over them helplessly, one fact clearly emerged. Nearly all of his clients still owed Claude Alacoque money. Somehow she would have to get hold of it.

The timid, gently-bred widow was not a good bill collector. She would spend days and nights driving over rough, mired roads, to the home of some debtor, only to be put off with a vague promise of "next month," or "something on account" or "you'll hear from us shortly."

The older boys had gone off to school at the Benedictine Abbey of Cluny. The younger boys had been sent to stay with their uncle Antoine, the parish priest. Madame Alacoque was afraid to leave Margaret home alone in the care of her dreadful in-laws, while she herself was out on the weary bill-collecting. So she sent the little girl to the boarding school of the Urbanist nuns of Charolles.

Margaret quickly became a pet of the kind sisters and a favorite of her classmates. But much as they loved her, they could not quite figure her out. One minute she would be organizing a hair-raising game of leapfrog or winning a round of checkers. The next minute she would be gone and would be found hours later off by herself in a corner somewhere, completely absorbed in prayer.

"There is something unusual in Margaret," her teacher said one day to the superior of the convent. "She seems to have some sort of special relation with God—and to be very much afraid that someone will find it out."

"I know, Sister," said the superior. "I've been watching her!"

"Mother," said the nun impulsively, "why don't we let Margaret make her first Communion? I know that she is much too young. But it would mean so much to her!"

Exactly what it meant to her the sisters never knew.

One of the outstanding characteristics of St. Margaret Mary's life was her overwhelming love for and hunger for the Blessed Sacrament. The seed of this love was sown on the day of her first Communion. It was a turning point in her life and she knew it was, even though she was a child. Later she wrote: "This Communion cast a great shadow of bitterness over all my little pleasures and games, so that I could not enjoy them anymore, although I sought them out eagerly. But when I wanted to play with my friends, I kept feeling something pulling me away, calling me. . . ."

Soon after her first Communion Margaret was stricken with a terrible, wasting sickness, probably some form of tuberculosis. Whatever it was, there was nothing in those days that any doctor could do for her. She lost so much weight that her bones seemed to be piercing her skin. It was agony to move her swollen joints. By the time her mother had brought her home to Verosvres, she was so weak that she could not walk a step without falling.

Although Margaret could not leave her bed, she knew that something was very wrong in the household. Her mother had not taken her to her old room in her parents' half of the estate, but to a little closet of a bedroom in the farm building, in-law territory. But although her relatives were so near, not one of them came to visit her.

For two years Margaret hung on in this sad state—neither living nor dying. Her own sufferings were nothing to her, compared with those she knew her mother was going through on her account. One day as Madame Alacoque knelt by the bed saying the Rosary with the sick girl, she suddenly broke off in the middle of a Hail Mary and said, "My little one, we have tried every other way! Why do you not promise the Blessed Mother, whom you love so well, that if she cures you, you will be one of her daughters?"

Margaret turned her pinched face toward her mother and smiled. "Oh yes," she said. "I will!" —and did.

A half-dead child in a little farm in Burgundy makes a vow to become a nun if she is cured of her illness. It seems a most insignificant moment of history. But it was the first step in one of God's most powerful and far-reaching plans for the sanctification of His Church.

Margaret fell asleep. For the first time since she had come home, she slept all night. Half awake the next morning, she tried to figure out what was different in the room. Something had changed. But what? Cautiously she sat up in bed. It was the first time in a year that she had done so without help. The difference, she realized, was in herself. She put her feet on the floor and stood up, hardly believing that her legs would hold her. She felt no pain at all, no sensation except the harmless prickling of pins-and-needles up and down her legs. She had just taken her first step when the door opened and her mother came in, carrying a cup of warm milk. She took one look at her daughter's radiant face and realized what had happened.

"Well, well, my fine lady! So you've got bored with lying about in bed! And high time, too!"

"I always *knew* she was just trying to get out of her share of the work!"

"I trust that a girl who's been cured by the Blessed Virgin Mary won't feel herself too holy to carry slops out to the pigs!"

Three faces, three pairs of eyes followed Margaret around the kitchen. It was like passing from one bad dream into another. Now for the first time in four years she realized what had been going on in her mother's household. It was no longer her mother's. Madame Alacoque was an unwelcome boarder, a poor relation, in the home of her in-laws. They had always despised her. Now they were in a position to do something about it.

Claude Alacoque's relatives had simply taken over the management of the estate. Until her eldest son came of age, there was not a thing Madame Alacoque could do about it. Margaret's uncle, Toussaint de la Roche, was her legal guardian.

Three women ran Toussaint's house for him, and what a threesome they were! There was his wife, Aunt Benoite, Claude Alacoque's sister. There was Toussaint's mother, who was called Great-Aunt Chappendye. Worst of all, there was old *Grand'mère* Alacoque herself—Claude's mother. How little resemblance there was between Margaret's father and his mother! Poor Madame Alacoque, so gentle and so helpless, was no match for the three cruel women who now ruled the household.

For years Margaret's illness had greatly annoyed these three ladies. They bitterly resented the little food that her mother managed to sneak from the kitchen to the sick room. Now that Margaret was suddenly well again and could take up her share of the household chores, they decided that she would make up for lost time!

Even when she was at home, timid Madame Alacoque could do little to protect Margaret. And when she was out on her pathetic rounds of bill-collecting, which had been interrupted by Margaret's illness, the poor girl was completely at the mercy of the three women.

One morning during the octave of the Annunciation, Margaret woke up before dawn and got out of bed. She was planning to go to Communion on this day, and as she said her prayers she could feel her heart beating fast with happiness. She looked out the window into the pale sunrise of late winter and rose from her knees. It was time to go.

She walked into the kitchen noiselessly, hoping

that she could find her bonnet and cloak and escape before anyone saw her. It was just before six. The household, she knew, was already up and around. She could hear Aunt Benoite's sharp voice yelling at the servant girl. "What have you done with the other egg, you thieving wench?"

"I tell you I brought in all I found!"

"Then go back and find another one or you'll not eat a mouthful this day!"

Margaret tiptoed over to the big clothes cupboard and pulled the handle. It was locked. Her aunt spun around and looked at her narrowly. "*Well*, it's about time her ladyship deigned to make an appearance. What are you looking for?"

"Please, Aunt," said Margaret, swallowing hard. "If I could have my cloak and bonnet, I'd like to go to Mass. I'll hurry back at once," she added quickly.

"Go to *Mass*?" Benoite echoed shrilly. "If you like the morning air so well you could be out feeding the chickens with your poor Aunt Catherine! Or—"

"*Maman! Maman!*" Four-year-old Antoine appeared at the doorway, his mean little face beaming with honest pride. "Lucette *did* hide the other egg. I spied on her!"

"Ah, that wretched girl!" Aunt Benoite rushed for the door.

"But Aunt—" Margaret said, desperation over-coming fear. She could hear the Angelus ringing already. But if she ran all the way, she would still be on time.

"Ask your Aunt Chappendye," Benoite flung over her shoulder.

"Please Aunt," said Margaret, "I want to go to Mass. May I have my cloak?"

"Mass?" Aunt Chappendye shrugged. "What do I care? You'll have to ask your grandmother, though."

Grandmother Alacoque, enthroned before the roaring fire, stopped rocking and looked up. As usual, she had not missed a word. She consid-ered the request briefly, then shook her head. "No reason to go to Mass," she said. "Not Sun-day."

"Oh, but Grandmother!" Margaret flew across the room and seized the scrawny hand. "It's the octave of the Annunciation and I just thought—" She stopped. How could she tell any of these people that her constant longing for Our Lord in the Blessed Sacrament pulled her to the church like a magnet?

"Not a holyday of obligation!" Grandmother announced triumphantly. "Besides, every time you go to Communion you moon around the whole day like an idiot and don't do a stitch of work!"

There was a loud screech from the courtyard. Benoite came in holding the missing egg aloft in one hand and dragging the weeping girl with the other. "There, you thief," she shrieked. "Now get to work on those clothes and don't try a trick like that again or you'll *really* be sorry!" She turned to Margaret, who was finally shedding great tears. "And just what are *you* sniveling about?"

"She's crying because she can't go to Mass," Aunt Chappendye said, giggling.

Benoite looked at her niece in genuine amazement. "*Crying because she can't go to Mass?* Why would anybody cry because of not getting to Mass?" Suddenly she threw back her head and roared with shrill, coarse laughter. She strode across the room and shook her finger under Margaret's nose. "You've got a date to meet some boy! That's why you're crying!"

"Oh Aunt!" Margaret began, her cheeks flaming. "You know that I—"

"Don't talk back to me, girl!" Aunt Benoite drew back her horny hand and delivered a stinging blow to the ear.

The room began to spin. Margaret turned and ran blindly out of the house. The feel of the cold

morning air against her skin cleared her mind
somewhat. Mastering her sobs, she ran like a
frightened young rabbit to the end of the farm-
yard and scrambled through the little woodland
that bordered it. At the bottom of the hill was a
large moss-covered rock. It was Margaret's favorite spot. Behind it she was invisible to all passers-
by. It was here that she came, whenever she could
escape, to think and to pray.

Across the valley Margaret could see the steeple
of the village church. Mass must be nearly over
now. Perhaps at this very moment the Communion
bell was ringing.

The evening Angelus was ringing when Margaret lifted her head and looked at the church
once more before leaving the shelter of the rock.
The red sanctuary lamp was visible now, through
the early dusk. She had kept vigil before it all
day—from a mile away.

Numb with cold and hunger, Margaret trudged
home. She would have considered herself lucky
if she had been given a tin cup and told to go beg-
ging for a living. She crept noiselessly into the
room she had left so happily that morning. Falling on her knees before the crucifix, she burst into
bitter sobs.

This was the life she led for the next four years.
Before it ended there would be more sorrow—the

worst sorrow that the mother and daughter had yet known. Madame Alacoque had lived on the knowledge that eventually her oldest son would come of legal age. Then he would return from school to take his place as head of the household. The happy day came, but the happiness was short. Jean died suddenly, at the age of twenty-three. The same terrible tragedy was repeated a year later, when the second son, Claude, came home and then died at the same age as his brother.

As they walked home from the graveyard after this second funeral, Madame Alacoque said between sobs, "My child, if the Blessed Mother had not answered our prayers—if she had taken you to heaven, and me after you, how much better off we would be! For what has she spared us? I cannot believe that we will ever again be happy in this life!"

TWO • "IT IS HERE THAT I WANT YOU—"

"Beautiful! Absolutely beautiful!"

Madame Alacoque was so happy at the sight that she laughed out loud. "It's perfect. Come to the mirror and see!"

Margaret ran across the room in a swirl of velvet and taffeta.

"Wait—let me pin the rose higher on the skirt. . . . There! Isn't it lovely? Blue is your color!"

"Blue will be everybody's color if you don't look out for the paint!" Chrysostome Alacoque swept his mother and sister out of the workman's path. "Now here," he said, pointing to the ceiling beam, "the Alacoque coat of arms. And here a pair of Cupids dancing, and here—"

"Oh, Madame," the painter interrupted, turning to the mother, "it does my heart good to see this old house made so beautiful again, and to see such happy young people in it!"

Madame Alacoque sighed happily. "Yes," she said, "almost as it was in the old days."

Chrysostome, the third son, was home to stay. He was of age. He was the master of the house. He was in robust health. Grandmother Alacoque and Aunt Chappendye had died and gone to their eternal rewards. Aunt Benoite was still very much alive. With Chrysostome around, however, she had to mind her manners as she had not minded them in years.

Chrysostome was getting married. That was why the house was being redecorated. Angelique, his bride-to-be, was the daughter of a nobleman. She was used to fine houses.

To Margaret and her mother it was like the end of a nightmare. The old house was once again filled with the sounds of gayety and laughter. Young folks from all over the countryside came calling on the Alacoques. Chrysostome's school companions and the elegant young friends of his fiancée became regular visitors at L'Hautecour.

To the delight of Madame Alacoque it soon became clear that the greatest attraction in the house was not really Chrys at all. It was Margaret. She was eighteen and very lovely, although her face, with its high, delicate cheekbones and great dark eyes, still showed some traces of the suffering she had undergone. Besides being beautiful, she was comfortably well to do. Uncle Toussaint de la Roche, for all his failings, had been a good manager. The farm was prospering and the Alacoques' affairs had been put in order. Margaret had a generous dowry. Together with her good looks, good family, and good disposition, it made her one of the most eligible girls for miles around.

Madame Alacoque began to make plans. She was not really happy about her son's marriage. For ten years she had lived at the mercy of other women. "Angelique is sweet enough," she said to herself. "But one never knows what a new daughter-in-law will be like once she's taken over the keys of the household!" It worried her. But if Margaret, her own girl, the only happiness in her life for so many years—if Margaret had her own husband and household!

"Weddings are happy times, my little one,"

Madame Alacoque said as she fitted the lace bodice of Margaret's ball gown. "I am happy for Chrysostome, of course. But the day I wait for and pray for is the day you wear a wedding gown!" She felt her daughter's arm stiffen under her fingers.

"But Mother—" They had been through this so many times before. "How *can* I marry? How can you forget the vow that we made, you and I together, that if the Blessed Mother would cure me I would be—"

"Child, child, you were so young and so ill when you made that vow! We could easily be dispensed from it. Your Uncle Antoine says so, and he is a priest and should know! Surely you can't be expected to shut yourself up in a convent now, when you're free and happy for the first time in years!"

Poor Margaret! She was plunged from one kind of misery into another. Now that her mother was safe with Chrysostome, Margaret saw no reason at all why she should not fulfill her vow— and her own great desire—by entering the convent. The trouble was that not one other person in the family agreed with her.

"What's got into you, Margaret?" Uncle Antoine, the parish priest of the village, asked her. "You don't have to run off to the convent to do the will of God! Your duty is to stay right here and take care of your mother. After all she's been through—"

"Really, Margaret," Chrysostome said. "You're not strong enough for that kind of life. Besides, how can you think of running off and leaving Mother? After all she's been through—"

Her brother Jacques, who was studying for the priesthood, had more subtle arguments. "The religious life is not for you, Margaret. I know all about the good works you're always doing secretly for the poor folks in the village. Who would take care of them if you went away? And how about the hours you spend praying and the extra penances you try to keep so secret? You wouldn't be allowed to do anything like that in the convent, you know. You're better off in the world."

When she was alone in her room at night another voice was added to the voices of her family. "You poor, miserable creature! What are you thinking of, wanting to become a religious?" Although she knew it was the voice of the devil, she could not shut it out of her ears. "You'll make yourself a laughingstock to the world. Where will you go when you've left the convent? For you certainly won't be able to persevere!" Margaret was so unsure of herself and her own worth that she heartily agreed with him.

As for Madame Alacoque, the mere mention of the word convent was enough to send her into floods of tears.

Margaret kept catching her mother and brother in earnest conversations that stopped abruptly when she came into the room. Then Madame Alacoque would say, "The great-nephew of the Baronne Desprès—your dear brother's godmother —is visiting next week for the carnival ball, my sweet. It is a fine family and they say that the young man has great charm." Or "I hear that the young Count de Bragelonne remains a bachelor because he does not care for these modern girls— too flighty, not serious or devout enough—" Or, "I'm retrimming your green velvet gown for the ball, my sweet. I'm sure you'll be the prettiest girl there. Oh, by the way, Madame Rivière told me that her cousin from Paris is down for the shooting season—"

"Well," Margaret thought at such moments, "why not?" Surely it would be better to make her mother happy by marrying than to disgrace the family by being asked to leave a convent. So she would put on the newly trimmed gowns and the elegantly plumed hats and go to meet the latest young man her mother had picked out, and there was much whispering in the drawing rooms about how much of a dowry that charming Mademoiselle Alacoque was expected to bring.

Margaret enjoyed the social life. She loved company and she liked having a good time as much as any other high-spirited girl. Madame Alacoque wavered between joy and despair. At parties she watched proudly while Margaret laughed and talked with the other young people. But by the next day something had happened. Margaret would come out of her room early, haggard and red-eyed, go to Mass, and then slip away for hours at a time, to that godforsaken spot where she went to pray, her mother knew. Madame Alacoque could tell by the look on her face that the idea of that convent was with her again.

What *happened* to Margaret after those gay evenings, she wondered.

Neither her mother nor anyone else could ever have guessed. Oh, of course everyone knew that she was devout and spent more time praying than seemed quite necessary to her family. But no one suspected the unbelievable truth about Margaret. If she had told them that she was in direct and frequent communication with Our Lord, they would have said, "Imagination!"

Not even Margaret herself understood it. She was so humble that she thought her experiences must be shared by nearly everybody else. Coming back to her room after a gay party, she would find a visitor waiting for her.

"My sovereign Master appeared before me, as He had been in His scourging, all disfigured, overwhelming me with strange reproaches: that it was my vanities which had reduced Him to this state, and that I was wasting a time so precious of which He would demand from me a rigorous account at the hour of death."

To take her mind off the terrible struggle, she spent most of her time caring for the poor and sick of the village. The children of these families worried her most of all. The little ones, left on their own, ran wild over the fields all day until they grew big enough to lift a hoe and take over their share of the work. It never occurred to anyone to teach them to say their prayers or catechism. Bribing them with candy, Margaret gathered the poorest and dirtiest of the village children, and taught them what she could. When the weather grew too cold to hold class in the fields, she tried to sneak them into her room. She might have succeeded if Aunt Benoite's sharp eyes had not spotted a suspicious number of muddy footprints leading to Margaret's door.

"Ah, sacré bleu! Look at my floor! Get this

bunch of ragamuffins out of here, you lazy, worthless girl! *Out!*"

The children tumbled out of Margaret's room and fled.

"I'll clean the footprints, Aunt," Margaret stammered.

"*You'll* clean them! You've never yet cleaned a floor clean!" Aunt Benoite muttered, sweeping furiously. She longed to bring the broom down over Margaret's head, but Chrysostome was within hearing. "You're good for nothing except to bring in a wealthy husband, and even *that* you won't do!"

Chrysostome had watched the parade of children with some surprise. "What's this, Margaret?" he asked. "Do you mean to become a schoolteacher?" He laughed through his annoyance. What would Angelique think of *this*!

Little works of charity were no real answer to the terrible ferment in Margaret's heart. One day—after the battle had been raging for six years—it was all settled. While she prayed after Communion, Our Lord simply asked Margaret point-blank to give up the struggle against Him. . . . "*We must be faithful to each other, you and I*" . . . From that day on the timid girl lost all her doubts. She stopped being afraid. She asked her mother and brother to say a final no, thank you, to all her suitors. "I will never, never give up the idea of entering a convent," she said firmly.

Madame Alacoque saw that her tears no longer had an effect, so she stopped crying and tried one last delaying tactic. Margaret was sent to visit her mother's brother in the near-by town of Mâçon. What Madame Alacoque did not know was that Uncle Philibert secretly sympathized with Margaret's desire to be a nun. His own daughter was in an Ursuline convent in the town. "That's where you belong, Margaret. Your cousin will be with you, and your mother won't worry so much knowing that I'm right here keeping an eye on you."

Margaret smiled. "Dear Uncle," she said, "you're so good. But I can't enter the Ursuline house. I know how wonderful the Ursulines are, but if I entered the convent here it would be because I love you and my cousin. I want to go somewhere where I have no friends, no relatives —nobody but God." She wrinkled her smooth brow. "Do you understand?"

"Frankly, no. Besides, your brother is going to be difficult about your dowry, you know. If you enter the Ursuline convent I can make special arrangements about the payments." Margaret shook her head vigorously. "Well, then, where do you want to go?"

"To Sainte-Marie!"

This was the popular name given to the Order of the Visitation. It had been founded sixty years before by St. Francis de Sales and a saintly widow named Jane de Chantal. Margaret did not know exactly why she felt so strongly attracted to this order, unless it was because Visitation nuns were called "Daughters of Mary."

A few days later Chrysostome arrived unexpectedly to bring Margaret home. Their mother was very sick and was calling for her. "You see, Margaret," he said reproachfully, "she cannot bear even to have you gone a few days! How can you talk of leaving her forever?"

It began all over again. But Margaret had finished arguing with them. She simply waited. Had not Our Lord Himself agreed to arrange things for her?

He managed it in this way. In the year 1670 the Holy Father proclaimed a jubilee year. Soon special preachers were traveling all over France to spread the word. The Alacoque home was the largest in Verosvres, and the Franciscan friar who was preaching in that part of the country stayed at L'Hautecour for several days.

This was the first real spiritual direction that Margaret had ever had. The Franciscan realized at once that there was something unusual here.

After a few talks with Margaret he was certain that she had a true vocation. "Why does your brother stand in your way?" he asked her.

Margaret lowered her eyes. "I think—he—would find it inconvenient to pay my dowry just now."

The priest sighed so softly that Margaret did not hear him. He was sure that Chrysostome Alacoque would have produced the dowry quickly enough if it had been for a wealthy marriage. Did the man really have so little idea of what a pearl was buried in this field? "I will speak to him," the Franciscan said.

"Are you really and truly determined to do this, Margaret?" Chrysostome asked.

"Oh, Chrys," said Margaret, her eyes filling with tears, "I would rather die than change!"

"Well then—all right. I'll go to see the Ursulines at Mâcon. Our uncle says—"

"No, Chrys, I want to go to a Visitation convent."

Chrysostome shrugged. If she were really determined to do this foolish thing, it did not really matter where she went. "Well—there is a Visitation convent at Dijon, and one at Lyons, and one at Paray-le-Monial, and one at—"

"At Paray-le-Monial!"

The name rang a bell in her heart. She did not know why.

The coach rumbled along the old Roman road that led from Charolles to Paray. As it passed the ancient shrine of Our Lady of Romay, Margaret stuck her head out of the window and caught her first view of the little town that lay at the foot of the hill. Rich green meadows stretched out on either side of the road, rolling back to the gentle Burgundian hills. Margaret was so excited by the sight of the town that she had no interest in admiring the lovely view she could have seen by turning her head.

"Chrys! What are those great steeples?"

"The Benedictine abbey," Chrys said without having to look. "Highest thing in the town. And your little convent is right underneath it, practically in its shadow."

The coach stopped at the Paray gate to let off the two passengers. Margaret all but danced through. "Hurry, Chrys—*do* hurry!" she called over her shoulder.

"Have a little patience, Margaret," he muttered, wiping the sweat from his face. He lumbered after his light-footed sister, wondering how the girl could take such delight in a place that was this hot so early in the afternoon.

The Visitation convent stood on the rue de la Saulnerie. Margaret reached it well in advance of her brother and stood peering anxiously into the open doorway of the chapel, until she heard Chrys huffing and puffing up the hill. "You've waited long enough for this, Margaret," he said, ringing the bell. "You *could* wait a few seconds more until I catch my breath."

Chrysostome had been making gruff remarks all morning, in the belief that it was better to make gruff remarks than to burst into tears, which was what he really felt like doing. Margaret straightened her bonnet nervously and smoothed the fingers of her gloves.

In a few minutes the door was opened by a white-veiled lay sister who invited them into the parlor and promised to send the mother superior immediately. When she was out of earshot Chrysostome looked over the simple, whitewashed room, and said, "Well, no one could accuse them of extravagance anyway!"

Margaret did not hear him. She was listening with all her attention to another voice, much more real than her brother's. The voice said: "*It is here that I want you to be!*"

She sank down on one of the hard wooden chairs and sighed gently. For the first time in fifteen years she felt completely at peace with the world. "Now remember," she heard Chrys saying, "we're here to look the place over, *not* to make any final arrangements, so—"

"But we *must* make the arrangements," Margaret said, "because I will go no place but here!"

Before he could answer, the curtain on the other side of the grille was opened and two nuns appeared. "Good afternoon, Monsieur Alacoque," said one of them. "I am Mother Hersant. Good afternoon, Mademoiselle."

Margaret curtsied and smiled through the grille at the two black-veiled women. The mother superior said, "May I present Mother Marie Thouvant, our mistress of novices." She smiled kindly at Margaret's flushed face. "Am I right in supposing that this visit concerns our mistress of novices?"

"Oh yes, *ma très honorée Mère!*" Margaret blurted out. "I am praying and praying that I will be accepted as a novice here!" She did not even feel Chrysostome's elbow nudge her arm.

After a little talk with the would-be novice, Mother Hersant asked her to step into another parlor and chat with some of the other nuns, so that she and Chrysostome could get down to the business details. Margaret, usually so shy and quiet, could hardly talk quickly enough to say all that she wanted to say to her companions across the grille. Two of the older nuns exchanged a disapproving look. The girl seemed a bit frivolous, did she not?

In those days there were no application blanks and psychological tests and school transcripts to be filled out and presented before obtaining permission to enter a convent. The fact that Madame Fautrières, whose daughter was in this very convent, was Margaret's godmother was a strong enough recommendation. Mother Hersant and Chrysostome quickly settled the financial arrangements. Chrysostome was groaning inside at the thought of parting with Margaret's dowry.

"When may we expect your dear sister?" Mother Hersant finally asked.

"As soon as her affairs at home are settled. I'm afraid," he added half-grudgingly, "that no matter how short the time it will seem all too long to Margaret."

"This is the twenty-fifth of May. Shall we say —the twentieth of June?"

As the convent door shut behind the Alacoques, Mother Hersant smiled at the novice mistress and said, "I have a feeling, Mother, that our new postulant is quite an extraordinary girl."

Mother Thouvant smiled. "I hope, dear Mother, that she will not be *too* extraordinary. Extraordinary novices can be a terrible trial!"

Margaret's last weeks at home were the happiest she had spent since her childhood. Even Madame Alacoque could not help catching some of her daughter's happiness. She no longer wept at the mere thought of June 20. Margaret felt as though she were dancing her way through the days that separated her from Paray. She wore her most beautiful clothes and jewels. She accepted every invitation to every party and was the merriest guest at all of them. Watching her drive off in the carriage with Angelique and Chrysostome, Aunt Benoite muttered, "Look at that vain girl in her laces and velvet! She certainly looks and behaves like a nun, doesn't she?"

Aunt Benoite would have been the last person in the world to understand that Margaret's joy and gayety was that of a bride getting ready for her wedding day.

On Saturday, June 20, 1671, she left for Paray-le-Monial.

"At last came that day, so long desired, of saying farewell to the world. Never had I felt such joy or firmness in my heart. . . . For I felt like a

slave who feels herself delivered from prison and chains, to enter the house of her beloved."

"Let's say good-by out here, Chrys," Margaret said, at the gate of the courtyard. "I think it will be easier if you don't come in—"

He nodded, unable to say a word. Margaret rang the bell and waited, her knees weak and her lip trembling. What had become of her gayety and joy? This was the day for which she had waited all her life. Why was she suddenly afraid of what she was doing?

Margaret had no way of knowing that what she was feeling at this moment had been felt many times before—by nearly everyone who has ever entered the cloistered convent. She longed to turn her head and look at her brother, but she knew that if she did, she would simply rush back to him and say, "Take me home!"

The door opened.

Mother Hersant's experienced eye immediately took in the tense white face and the trembling lip. "Come in, my dear child—and welcome home," she said.

Margaret stepped inside. The door closed silently behind her. As she followed the superior through the grille that separated the front hall from the cloister, she steeled herself against the terrible fear—and found that it had disappeared. She could not even remember what it had felt like. All she could do was repeat over and over again in her heart the one sentence that made any sense to her at all.

"It is here that I want you to be!"

THREE · A BLANK CANVAS

In the middle of the seventeenth century, a terrible religious doctrine called Jansenism began to grow. It taught that Our Lord had not died for all men but only for a chosen few; that Holy Communion was not for everyone, but only for the near-perfect, and that frequent Communion was wrong even for them; that man was by nature too vile to deserve the love of God.

Three hundred years later it is hard to believe

that these blood-chilling ideas were ever seriously held by Catholics. But they were. Jansenism spread rapidly throughout France and the neighboring countries, in spite of strong opposition both from the Pope and the King of France. And wherever it spread, the fervor of the people grew colder, as Communions became less and less frequent. What had gone out of religion in those days, at least for those affected by Jansenism, was the idea of love. It was as though the lifeblood of the Church were slowly freezing up.

In heaven a magnificent plan was made to thaw it out. God was preparing to give to mankind a living symbol of His burning love—a symbol of love that has as much meaning for us today as it would soon have for the Catholics of seventeenth-century France.

As the apostle of this fiery revolution God had not chosen a learned, eloquent prince of the Church, with powerful friends in Rome. On the contrary. It was as though He had searched the world for the most obscure, the most humble, the least forceful messenger He could find to entrust with the mission. He had found Margaret Mary Alacoque. The first step in the plan was now complete. God had Margaret exactly where He wanted her.

The convent building and its huge garden extended nearly four blocks. The novitiate was in a tower, separated from the main building by a passageway. Mother Thouvant led the newcomer to her cell and opened the door. "Here we are, my child. This will be yours for a year. We change our cells and our possessions every year to avoid forming attachments to them."

The little room was simple but spotless. "Oh, how beautiful it is!" Margaret said. She could see how one could become attached to a place of such peace and order. Best of all was the comfortable-looking four-poster bed, with its glowing white canopy and covers.

"Our holy founder, St. Frances de Sales, did not think that a nun must sleep on a plank or eat roots in order to be holy," said Mother Thouvant. She had caught the look of surprise on Margaret's face. "He did not want his daughters to wear out their bodies by long fasts or midnight prayers. Now dear, see how quickly you can change into your black dress and bonnet. Your sisters are all eagerly waiting to meet you."

Margaret's hands were trembling so hard that she could hardly tie the bow of her close-fitting bonnet. But soon she was following Mother Thouvant into the sunny room where the novices were waiting for her. The three girls could not hide their excitement and curiosity as they greeted the newcomer who was joining them at the advanced old age of twenty-three.

Sister Anne Piednuz was eighteen. Sister Françoise-Catherine du Chailloux was fifteen. Sister Anne Rosselin was fourteen. She had come to the convent school when she was seven. This year she had literally talked her way into the novitiate—six months before the legal age.

The bell rang. "Now, my dear children, I am going to leave our postulant in your care during recreation. You may show her the garden, and tell her whatever you can about our convent and our life here."

The girls were delighted with the idea of having Margaret all to themselves. They hurried her off to the garden, all talking at once.

"The lilies are our special pride," said Sister du Chailloux, "and Sister Marie-Bénigne says they have never been tended so beautifully as by us novices."

"Sister Marie-Bénigne arranges the flowers for the altar," explained one of the other girls. She pointed to a beautiful nun who was walking across the garden. Margaret had never seen her godmother's daughter. She looked after the tall, stately figure with some curiosity.

"And that is Sister Madeleine des Escures next

to her," one of the girls said. "She is the most perfect nun imaginable! Our mistress says that she is the living rule, and that we should imitate her as much as we can!"

"And there goes Sister Marest carrying fresh berries to the infirmary for her patients. She is such a jolly and kind nurse that it's almost a pleasure to be sick."

"And that very handsome sister coming across the cloister?" asked Margaret.

"Oh, that is Sister de Sirot," said Sister Rosselin. "She is—uh—of a very noble family."

"How wonderful they all look!" exclaimed Margaret, eyeing the black-veiled figures with naïve awe. "I just know they are all saints!"

"I am *sure* our superior is a saint!" little Sister Rosselin announced breathlessly, nodding her head so hard that her white veil flew out behind her. "She is from Paris and for twenty years her spiritual director was the saintly Father Vincent de Paul."

"And Mother Thouvant, our mistress of novices!" Sister Piednuz said. "She was the first nun to be professed at Paray. Her father helped to found our convent—in 1626. Our convent is one of the oldest in our order," she added, as proudly as though she herself had placed the cornerstone.

"And when she was a very young nun," Sis-

ter Rosselin said, "our holy Mother de Chantal
blessed her and said that she would be a great
value to the order. Imagine," she sighed happily,
"having really *seen* our blessed Mother de Chantal!"

The girls chattered on. Their earnest little faces
beamed with pride at every word they said about
their convent. "How kind they are," Margaret
thought. "And how happy!" Out loud she said,
"You are all so fortunate to have come here so
young. I'm afraid I will never learn when and
how to do everything properly."

"Oh, but dear Sister," said Sister Rosselin, "of
course you will learn! There is nothing to it. We
rise at five, go to chapel at 5:30, leave it at 6:45
for our household tasks; at eight we return to
chapel for the little hours, hear Mass at 8:30, do
our chores at 9:30, eat dinner at ten, and have
recreation at eleven. At noon we rest for half an
hour, do our work until two, sing Vespers at
three and have a conference on our reading at
3:30. At five we sing Compline, have prayers at
5:20, finish up the day's tasks at 5:50. Supper and
recreation at 6:05; meeting at eight for the reading of the next day's gospel and epistle. At 8:22
assignment of the next day's task. Beginning of
the great silence at 8:30. Matins and Lauds at
8:45. Leave choir at 9:30. All in bed by ten."

Sister Rosselin gasped for breath, then beamed. "You see, Sister, the schedule's really very simple!"

Margaret did not know whether to laugh or cry. She was saved from having to choose by the sound of the bell. Mother Thouvant came across the grass smiling. "I shall use this time to explain our system of meditation to you, my dear. You'll find that it's really very simple—"

Margaret's heart sank down to her shoes.

Margaret fell asleep that night in a mixed-up haze of homesickness, happiness and confusion. She was awakened early next morning by the sound of a voice. It was as real as the sound of the rising bell that soon rang outside her door. The voice was saying something to her. But what? She would ask Mother Thouvant after morning prayers, she thought.

"Mother—"

"Yes, what is it, child?" Mother Thouvant happened to be in a great hurry on her way to the infirmary with some fruit. But she stopped and smiled at Margaret cordially.

"This morning when I woke up I heard a voice in my cell. It said—something I didn't quite understand. I'm so stupid about Latin. Something like '*Audi, Filia, et—et vide—*'"

This time it was Mother Thouvant's heart that sank. She said, "Come now, Sister, if you want to have long Latin dreams just before the bell rings, you won't have time to make your bed properly. You must have heard the words somewhere and forgotten that you knew them. They're from Psalm sixteen. You can look them up in your psalter."

Hear, O daughter, and see. . . . Forget thy people and thy father's house, for the King hath greatly desired thy beauty! Mother Thouvant said the words over to herself. "Oh dear," she thought, "this girl *is* going to be difficult after all!"

"Now, then," she said briskly, "how did the meditation go this morning?"

Margaret lowered her eyes. She did not know what to say. Meditation! How she had loved the word—without knowing exactly what it meant. But meditation, she had learned yesterday, did not consist of kneeling in chapel all lost in thoughts of her Beloved. There were set subjects on which to think, with points one, two and three, and a summing-up at the end. All this was designed to make the process simpler and more useful to the average person whose mind would wander unless it were well directed. But for Margaret, who for nearly all of her life had been in direct contact with heaven, it was hopeless. It was like asking an eagle to fly no higher than the perch of a canary's cage. In chapel that day Margaret had tried very hard to stay with points one, two and three, but once before the Blessed Sacrament her thoughts had simply risen to heaven and stayed there.

"Oh Mother," she said, "I did very badly. I'm very stupid about the meditation! Please, *please*, dear Mother—can you teach me to pray?"

Mother Thouvant did not yet know how unintentionally funny this request was, coming from Margaret. "My dear child," she said, trying not to sound cross, "you are entering the convent at the age of twenty-three! Do you really mean to tell me that you don't know how to pray?"

"It's true, Mother," said Margaret. "I don't."

Mother Thouvant thought for a moment and then said, "Go and place yourself in front of Our Lord like a canvas in front of a painter."

Margaret did not understand a word of this, but she was too timid to ask for any further explanation.

It came later. "Come, I will teach you!" Our Lord told her. When she was in the chapel, she writes, "My Sovereign Master made me see that my soul was the canvas on which He wished to paint all the aspects of His suffering life . . . and that He would make this impression after He had purified it from so much affection for the things of the world. . . ."

On August 25, the feast of the great St. Louis of France, the postulant was formally admitted to the novitiate. Madame Alacoque and the boys were there for the ceremony. Madame Alacoque had brought with her the beautiful white bridal gown and veil in which Margaret would appear briefly at the grille, before retiring to her cell to put on the holy habit.

In addition to the habit, Margaret would receive a new name. To her own she added her Confirmation name—"Mary," whose daughter she had once vowed to become.

As Margaret knelt before the grille, her face radiant in the candlelight, Madame Alacoque smiled through the happy tears that were running down her face. Her grief at Margaret's decision had changed to joy. How foolish she had been to resist the will of God so long, the mother thought. She remembered something she had said a long time ago: "But the day I wait for and pray for is the day you wear a wedding gown!"

The day had finally come.

"Mother Thouvant!" Sister Madeleine des Escures was on her way to the garden to gather some fruit for the sick sisters in the infirmary when she met the novice mistress. "I'm sure you don't need *my* poor advice on how to take care of your little chicks, but—uh—"

Mother Thouvant smiled. She knew what was coming. "But your advice is always welcome, Sister, and, frankly, in the case of the little Alacoque, I can use all the advice you have to give!"

Sister des Escures, whom the novices had described to Margaret as "the living rule," was really a very goodhearted person. But she had no patience with anybody who was *different*. The new novice most certainly was.

"I was watching her in chapel this morning," Sister des Escures said, wrinkling her brow in disgust at the mere thought of it. "After Communion she knelt as though she were made of marble, with a look on her face as though she were—well, seeing a vision of heaven, or something equally unlikely. She was definitely calling attention to herself and it does set *such* a bad example to the other novices. And she paid not the slightest attention when it was time to leave and the bell rang!"

Mother Thouvant sighed. "At times Sister Alacoque acts as though bells were rung in convents for the mere enjoyment of their sound!"

Sister Madeleine des Escures clucked disapprovingly. If there was one thing she felt strongly about, it was the prompt answering of bells!

"But I have seen this sort of thing before, Sister," the novice mistress went on. "Excess of zeal in a young novice is not unusual. Fortunately there is a sure cure." The two nuns had come to the spot in the garden where the novices were sewing and talking during recreation. "Sister Alacoque!" Mother Thouvant called. "Would you come here please?"

Margaret jumped up and hurried over, spilling her work basket in the process. "Gather up your sewing, Sister," said the novice mistress sharply. "We have no servants here to pick up after you!"

Margaret knelt down and collected her thimble and needle. Under the eyes of Mother Thouvant and the chilly stare of Sister des Escures she felt as though she had three thumbs on each hand. "Now then," said the novice mistress. "Tomorrow morning you may come into chapel for a few minutes to hear the points for meditation. Then you may leave the chapel and go sweep the cloister. After that I will give you your instructions for the rest of the day." Try as she would, Margaret could not keep a look of shocked surprise from crossing her face. The hours she could spend in the chapel already seemed so few. "Well, child," Mother Thouvant said, "you admit you can't master the rules of meditation anyway. So you might as well employ the time improving your household work, and get *something* learned properly!"

Every day after that Mother Thouvant had some extra chores ready and waiting for Margaret. While the other novices were in chapel, she was out sweeping the cloister, or washing down the steps of the novitiate, or weeding the garden. She felt as though she were starving for the presence of the Blessed Sacrament. When she gathered all her courage together one day and asked her mistress for a little more time in the chapel, Mother Thouvant said scornfully, "Really, Sister! It's a pity you can't pray while you work!"

Margaret, of course, *did* pray while she worked, and prayed in a way that Mother Thouvant did not even suspect. The girl's inner life was a complete mystery to her, to the other nuns, and to the rather dull-witted priest who acted as confessor to the convent. The effects of God's love for her had always been overpowering. Since the day she had received the habit they had become more and more marked. "The favors of divine love," she wrote, "were so excessive that they often carried me completely outside of myself and made me incapable of doing anything." One day she complained of this to Our Lord. "But if I *want* you to be deaf, dumb and blind in My presence, shouldn't you be content?" He asked her.

Deaf, dumb and blind in the almost continual presence of God! This was the girl who did not hear the bell calling her from chapel!

Knowing how it all turned out, it is easy, three hundred years later, to be very critical of Margaret's superiors. But we must remember that more people *think* they hear heavenly voices than actually *do* hear them. In those days less was known than is known today about how the mind works, and about how and why it sometimes plays tricks on perfectly honest people. Seventeenth-century novice mistresses had to be even more suspicious of such things than modern ones.

So Margaret did the chores while the other novices knelt in the chapel. As she worked she sang a little song that she had written:

"The more they thwart my love,
  The more my one Beloved sets me on fire.
  Let them afflict me day and night!
  They cannot take Him from my soul.
  The more sorrow I suffer,
  The more He will unite me to His Heart!"

In May of 1672 there was great excitement in the convent. A new superior was coming. Mother

Hersant's term of office was over. As she packed her few possessions for the journey to her new post, a disturbing thought crossed her mind. She had left the affairs of the Paray monastery in perfect order for Mother Suamaise, the next superior. But there was one piece of unfinished business for the newcomer to solve. What about Sister Alacoque? Should she be allowed to take her vows, after which it would be too late to get rid of her? Or should she be sent home to her family? Mother Hersant said a quick prayer of thanksgiving that she herself had been saved from having to make the decision.

It was no accident that sent Mother Saumaise to Paray at that particular moment. She was an ideal superior—kindhearted, levelheaded, open-minded. She was exactly what the situation called for. She listened to all the reports, complaints, and gossip about the convent's problem child, and thought, "I shall wait and see for myself." But she definitely approved of the plan to keep Margaret too busy with a broom to hear imaginary voices.

Before it is cast in its finished design, even the finest gold is put through the refiner's fire, so that even the tiniest particle of ore will be removed. Thus it was with Margaret. The mission that would soon be entrusted to her would take courage, and strength, and the faith that moves mountains. Her soul, already so strong and full of courage, was now undergoing the final preparation.

The mission had not yet been revealed. During the sad, discouraging days of her novitiate, she had the first hint of it. In chapel one day Our Lord said to her: "I seek a victim for My Heart who will sacrifice itself as an offering of immolation for the accomplishment of My designs!"

A victim for My Heart!

In the old law a victim was offered and was sacrificed to satisfy divine justice. Christ Himself had once been a victim, sacrificed to accomplish a great plan: the redemption of mankind. Now He Himself sought a being willing to sacrifice itself in order that some divine plan might be carried out.

It never occurred to the humble novice that she herself might be a part of this plan. She helpfully suggested the names of several of the holiest nuns. In the silence of the chapel the whispered answer echoed in her heart like distant thunder: *"I wish for no one else but you!"*

Margaret had been in the convent for more than a year. She had seen one of her fellow novices, Sister Piednuz, professed. She knew that there was no doubt that the other two novices would soon take their vows. But would *she*?

"Yet something *must* be decided soon," Mother Saumaise said to Mother Thouvant. "Sister Alacoque cannot remain a novice forever. Either she must take her vows, as the other girls are to do, or she must be sent home."

The meeting of Mother Saumaise's council had taken care of all the small subjects it had to discuss and had now come to the most difficult item on the list—Sister Alacoque.

"May I say a word, Mother?" said Sister des Escures.

"Certainly, Sister."

Sister Madeleine des Escures, whose back was already as straight as a beanpole, straightened it still further. "No one can deny that Sister Margaret Mary is an unusual and a—well—a *truly* good and devout girl! No one can deny that she is obedient and that she *tries* hard. The question is: does she belong in this convent?"

There was a moment of silence.

"Do you remember, Mother," the nun went on, "that our two holy founders once knelt together at the altar and prayed that our order would never be blessed with extraordinary graces? Well—" She shrugged ever so slightly. "Even if

Sister Margaret Mary is truly under some divine influence to act the way she acts, does she belong *here*?"

There was such terrible logic in the sister's speech that Mother Saumaise could think of no answer. She hesitated for a moment and then said to Mother Thouvant, "Go and tell Sister Alacoque that her profession is to be postponed indefinitely—and why."

"Alas, my Lord! You are the reason they are sending me away!"

Margaret knelt in the chapel, her eyes closed tight to keep the tears from rolling down her nose.

Mother Thouvant had delivered the message with a few touches of her own thrown in. "You are nowhere near the true spirit of the Visitation, child! Simple observance of the rule! That is all we ask of a novice. We simply have no place here for extraordinary transports and raptures! I think you had better write your mother and brother and prepare them for the possibility of your coming home!"

So it had really happened. Back in L'Hautecour she had heard the voice of Satan predicting this very thing: "Where will you go when you've left the convent? For you certainly won't be able to persevere!"

"Alas! my Lord," Margaret whispered again. "*You* are the reason they are sending me away!"

The answer that came to her was rather startling, but it was certainly practical. A few minutes later Sister Alacoque was knocking firmly on the superior's door. "May I speak to you for a moment please, Mother?" she asked. "I have a message for you."

Mother Saumaise blinked. "A message? What is it, Sister?"

"I told Our Lord what you said and He asked me to tell you that you have nothing to fear in receiving me for profession, and that He Himself will answer for me, and—" Her brow was wrinkled in her efforts to repeat the message exactly as she had been given it. "—and that if you think He is a good risk, He will be my guarantee!"

Mother Saumaise opened her mouth and closed it again. She was speechless. She looked into Margaret's earnest face and then turned away. The very boldness of the message—its polite but obvious sarcasm—suddenly convinced her. Timid little Sister Alacoque would not have dared to make up such a message, thought the superior.

Mother Saumaise was naturally shaken by this direct communication with Our Lord. But she held her ground. He would be Margaret's guarantee, Our Lord had said? Very well, then. He was the one who had suggested it! She said coolly, "Then tell Our Lord that for a mark of that guarantee, I would like Him to make you useful to holy religion by an exact—*exact*, mind you—observance of all the rules!"

Margaret bowed and slipped away. Mother Saumaise felt a great longing to put her head down on the desk and groan. She was not too surprised when Sister Alacoque, her face radiant, came back to say that everything was all right. Our Lord had agreed to the terms.

"I will make you more useful to religion than she thinks," He had said, "but in a way that is known only to Me . . . and I am content that you prefer the will of your superiors to Mine. . . . For Myself, I reserve only the direction of your interior life and particularly of your heart in which, having established the empire of My pure love, I will not yield to others."

Mother Saumaise threw up her hands. "Very well, then! If the bargain is kept, you may take your vows before the end of the year!"

From that day on the novice never missed a

bell. The date of her profession was set for November 6, 1672.

Before this ceremony Visitation nuns make a ten-day retreat which they call a "solitude." Margaret's retreat, however, was not exactly made in solitude. She had company. The convent owned two donkeys, mother and son. Even during her retreat, Margaret was in sole charge of them. Although she was not allowed to tie the animals up, she had strict orders not to let them loose in the vegetable garden. The garden, of course, was exactly where they most wanted to be. "All they did was run," she wrote later, "and I had no rest until the evening Angelus, when I went in to supper, and then I went back to the stable during a part of Matins to feed them. . . . Yet I was so happy at this work that I would have been content if it had lasted all my life!"

For here in the garden, alone except for the animals, uninterrupted by bells, unseen by curious eyes, Margaret enjoyed the constant company of Our Lord. He stayed by her side all day long and kept watch with her. . . . All of her life she remembered this spot in the garden as a place of special joy. "It was here that I received such graces as I had never experienced before. Especially what He made known to me on the mystery of His holy death and passion. But the depth of it is too great to write, and the length makes me silent on it. I will only say that it is this which has given me so much love for the Cross that I cannot live one moment without suffering. . . ."

On one of these days, when the two animals were even more hungry than usual, she tried to break off in the middle of a conversation with Our Lord to chase them out of the turnips.

"Oh, let them go," He told her. "They won't do any harm!"

There is a delightful tradition handed down through the years in the Paray monastery that some of the nuns who had seen the two animals picnicking through the vegetables, rushed down to give the novice a piece of their mind—and found not a hoofprint in the dirt and not a leaf gone or even out of place.

And at last came the day that Margaret had never really believed would come—November 6, 1672. Crowned with white flowers, she said at last the words she had so longed to say: "I, Margaret Mary, beg for the love of Our Savior to be received to holy Profession in the Congregation of Our Lady of the Visitation, to exercise all my life therein the divine service by Obedience, Chastity, and Poverty."

"How sweet are thy tabernacles, Lord God of hosts," sang the choir. "My soul hath longed for the courts of the Lord!"

The words echoed deep in her heart. No soul had ever longed for them more fervently.

FOUR • THE MISSION IS REVEALED

"There, Sister! *That's* the way you apply a poultice. You don't want it dripping down the patient's chin, do you?" Sister Marest was not many years older than Margaret, but she had a habit of explaining things to her in the slow, careful way one explains things to a child. "Now fetch me the verbena from the herb shelf and we'll brew some tea for poor Sister de Sirot's head.

It's the best thing there is for migraine. No, Sister
—not foxglove! *Verbena!*"

Sister Marest was the most efficient nun in the
convent. She had a brisk, no-nonsense manner
about her that made the patients in the infirmary
feel better. They felt, somehow, that their aches
and pains could not possibly stand up against
Sister Marest.

"Now, Sister, don't—*please* don't walk around
the bed so many times when you make it!" Sister
Marest hated to see anyone waste a second or a
step. "Finish it up on one side and then go around
to the other side. It's only common sense!"

Common sense, Sister Marest thought, was
what the newly professed Sister Alacoque lacked
above all else. She was a dear, sweet girl, the head
nurse thought, no doubt about that. And she
treated every sick person in the infirmary like the
Queen of France but—"Sister! Look where
you're going!" A pot of water fell to the floor
with a crash that made Sister de Sirot groan and
clutch her aching head.

It was hard. Sister Marest was kind, even when
she was scolding Margaret for some boner or
other. But she did not understand how difficult it
was for the newly professed sister to do her
everyday chores. Margaret wrote about her profession day: "I will merely say that He adorned

me and treated me like a bride of Thabor. . . .
From that time forward He allowed me continually to enjoy His Divine Presence, but in a
manner which I had not yet experienced. . . . I
saw and felt Him close to me and heard His voice
much better than if it had been with my bodily
senses."

It is easy to see why Margaret found it hard to
keep her wits about her while she was making
beds and mixing poultices. She was now the infirmary assistant. The superior had decided that
a few months with Sister Marest was just what
she needed.

"It's no wonder I'm businesslike," the head
nurse told Margaret one day. "My dear mother
had just returned from early Mass and opened
up her shop—and suddenly I was born, right at
the start of the business day! Sister, will you
please—!" She leaped across the room and
snatched up the water kettle which had just boiled
over and put out the fire. Margaret, who had been
lost in thought, started up quickly and murmured,
"Oh, Sister, I'm so sorry!"

Sister Madeleine des Escures sat up in bed and
looked at her sternly. Sister des Escures' bones
reacted to cold weather as faithfully as a ther-
mometer. By early December her rheumatism
was always going full-blast. Margaret blushed.

She knew exactly what the good sister was thinking at that moment.

"Never mind," said Sister Marest quickly, suddenly feeling sorry for Margaret. Sister des Escures sometimes made even *her* feel clumsy. "Just try to keep your mind on your work, Sister. Save your dreaming for nighttime." To cover Margaret's embarrassment, she kept talking. "Did I ever tell you about the time I was sleeping next to the corpse?"

Margaret's eyes opened wide. "No, Sister!"

"Well, there was a fearful epidemic in the town and it spread to the convent. One of our sisters had just died and I laid out her body. I wanted to catch a bit of sleep, but our superior was sick in the infirmary at that time and she was a very nervous superior indeed! I was terribly afraid that I would not hear her if she called me. So I said to the dear sister who had just died, 'Look here, Sister. All the beds are filled. I'll just lie down here next to you and see that you wake me up if our mother wants me!' With that I fell into a deep sleep. A little after midnight I felt a cold hand shaking my shoulder. I woke up at once and sure enough, the poor superior had been calling me and calling me! I rushed to her bed—but not before I turned to the corpse and said, 'Oh, such foolishness!'"

Margaret laughed. Even Sister des Escures smiled faintly. "Now, Sister," said the nurse, "I think Sister Madeleine could do with a warm bed. Just run this pan of hot coals down to the kitchen and heat them up a bit, since our fire's out."

Margaret seized the pan and hurried toward the stairs. "Such a sweet girl," Sister Marest said, sighing, "If only she were a bit less clumsy, she —*Holy Mother protect us!*" There was a fearful crash from the floor below! Sister Marest rushed down the stairs and found Margaret sitting dazed at the bottom of them. She had fallen the length of the worn, wooden steps, but had somehow managed to keep the live coals from scattering over the floor. Through the mixed scolding and sympathy of Sister Marest, Margaret could hear another voice—a voice almost choking with light, mocking laughter. "*Oh, you clumsy fool! You'll never do anything worth while!*"

The devil's redoubled efforts to do Margaret all the harm he could during these days was well-timed. She was on the brink of a discovery that would deal a mortal blow to him and his best interests. . . .

The cold, damp winter settled in. Sister Marest and her assistant were kept busy with a steady procession of rheumatism, pneumonia, and chil-

blains. Christmas came, and two days later, the
feast of St. John, the beloved apostle whose head
had rested on the Heart of Jesus. It was late on
the afternoon of December 27, 1673. During
the holy octave, a deep sense of peace had settled
over the convent. The infirmary, although filled
with patients, was unusually quiet. Sister Marest
and Margaret had made a hot spiced drink for
the sick sisters and most of them were napping.
Sister Marest looked at Margaret and suddenly
felt a great surge of pity. Poor girl! When had
anyone ever worked so hard to turn a natural-
born Mary into a Martha as she had done with
Margaret?

"Sister, dear," she said, "I don't need you for
the next few hours. All our sick folks are sleeping. If you'd like to go to the chapel for a bit,
go ahead!"

Margaret's eyes glowed. "Oh, Sister! Thank
you!" She almost ran out of the infirmary. Her
longing to be in the presence of the Blessed Sacrament was always intense but today it was stronger
than ever. All afternoon she had felt an irresistible
impulse to rush to the chapel—as though something were waiting for her there.

She hurried through the deserted garden. The
frost-covered grass glinted red and gold in the
setting sun. There was no sound in the garden

but the voices of the two lay sisters at the kitchen window, singing a Christmas hymn together, as they worked. The other nuns were all in the community room. The outside door, which admitted the people of the town to the main part of the chapel, was locked. Margaret was absolutely alone.

She knelt as close to the grille as she could, to be near the altar.

Even before she had fixed her eyes on the tabernacle, it seemed to Margaret that the guttering glow of the hundred red vigil lamps had begun to fade before a dazzling light that was streaming from the altar. She felt as though she were kneeling in a place that was outside of space and time, a place lost in the splendor of heaven. Before her stood Our Lord, and clearly visible in His Sacred Side, she saw His Heart.

". . . He made known to me the marvels of His love and the inexplicable secrets of His Sacred Heart, which He had kept hidden until then. He opened It to me for the first time, but in a manner so effective and real that He left no further room for doubt. . . . He said, 'My Heart is so inflamed with love for men and for you in particular, that no longer able to contain within Itself the flames of Its burning charity, It must spread them abroad, by means of you. . . . I have chosen you, as an abyss of unworthiness and ignorance, for the accomplishment of this great design. . . ."

Then, "Will you give Me your heart?" He asked.

"Oh, please take it!"

Inside the glowing Heart of Christ, she now saw her own heart—"a little atom that consumed itself in this burning furnace, from which drawing it out like a burning flame in the shape of a heart, He put it back in the place from which He had taken it, saying, 'There, my beloved, is a precious token of My love which locks in your heart a little spark of its living flames. . . .'"

When the bell rang and the other sisters filed into the chapel, they found Margaret kneeling alone by the grille, absolutely motionless. The chanting of the office began and still she did not move back to her own place in the rear of the chapel.

"Really," thought Sister des Escures, glancing at the burning cheeks and tightly shut eyes of the young nun, "what a spectacle Sister Alacoque makes of herself! I'm afraid she's worked herself up into a fever!"

The next few days were the hardest that Margaret had ever lived through. For, as she said, "after such a great favor and one which lasted for so long a time, during which I did not know whether I was in heaven or on earth, I remained for several days . . . so beside myself that I could scarcely utter a word without violence to myself. And I felt such a great fullness of God that I could not explain myself to my superior as I wanted to!"

In the weeks that followed, Margaret pondered in her heart the frightening words Christ had said to her. "*I have chosen thee . . . for the accomplishment of this great design!*"

Something was expected of her—of her, the girl who could not even tend a kettle of water or make a meditation the way she was supposed to make it. *She*, in some mysterious way, was supposed to handle the affairs of heaven on earth. But how?

The second great vision of the Sacred Heart came soon after. This time the Heart of Jesus— "brilliant as the sun and transparent as crystal" —seemed to be enthroned on a great mass of flames. Around It was a crown of thorns, and in the center, the wound of the centurion's spear glowed like a ruby.

Christ told her of His great longing to be loved perfectly on earth by those for whom He had given His life. As a proof of this, He would soon give to His cold-hearted creatures a living symbol of His own burning love for them: His Sacred Heart. For this reason He wished the image of this Heart to be exposed in public—"to touch the unfeeling hearts of men." He promised great blessings wherever this was done.

"These are the designs," He told her, "for which I have chosen you. This is why I have given you so many graces and have taken quite special care of you from your very cradle. I Myself have been your teacher and your director, only that I might prepare you for the accomplishment of this great design and confide to you this great treasure which I am showing you here."

To all this Margaret could make only one reply —the reply of St. Thomas, "My Lord and My God!" There was nothing else to be said. It was not yet the time to ask questions.

As you can imagine, Margaret's usefulness and cleverness around the infirmary was not improved by the soul-shattering events she was living through during these weeks. Finally Mother Saumaise took pity on Sister Marest and got her a new assistant. Margaret was put in charge of the few little girls who had been given to the care of the nuns by their families who hoped to develop a vocation in them. They were called "sisters of the little habit," and many of them went on to the novitiate when they reached the proper age.

This assignment was far more suited to Margaret's talents than the infirmary had been. Her kindness and gentleness to these little girls won their hearts immediately. For the first time Margaret found herself among people who accepted her as she was—and loved her for being that way. The little girls quickly figured out what the grownups in the convent had not yet realized. Naturally Sister Alacoque was different from other people. She was a saint. Other people were not saints. Therefore she was different from them. Often when she was kneeling in ecstasy in the chapel, they used to peek at her through the grille and call each other to see "how *our* saint is praying to God."

It was on the first Friday of some summer month of 1674 that Our Lord revealed to Margaret the next step in His great design. This time she was not alone. The community was gathered in the chapel for Benediction. The Blessed Sacrament was exposed on the altar. Margaret felt completely withdrawn into herself. She had no sooner knelt down at her place than the indescribable light that she had seen twice before surrounded her.

"Jesus Christ, my sweet Master, presented

Himself to me, all shining in glory, with His five wounds brilliant as five suns. . . ."

Once again Jesus spoke to her of His Heart's consuming love for mankind, from which He received in return so much ingratitude and coldness. "I feel this," He said, "more than everything I suffered in My passion! . . . If only they made Me some return of love, I would consider all that I have done for them as very little. . . . You, at least, make up for this ingratitude as much as you are able!"

And once again Margaret tried to tell Him that she felt too weak and too worthless for such a task.

"I will be your strength," He said. "Do not be afraid of anything, but listen carefully to My voice and do what I ask of you. . . ."

What He asked of her first was that she receive Communion as often as she was allowed to do so. In particular, she must do so on the first Friday of each month. And every Thursday night, He told her, He would let her share with Him the mortal sorrow that He knew in the Garden of Olives. "You must get up between eleven o'clock and midnight and remain prostrated for that hour . . . not only to appease the divine wrath . . . but also to lighten in some way the bitterness that I felt in being abandoned by My apostles. . . ."

When Benediction was over, the community rose and filed out of the chapel. Margaret remained in her place, seeing and hearing nothing, and unable to move. Here she knelt for hours, lost in the memory of what had happened.

The superior finally lost patience. She sent two of the other sisters to the chapel with orders to bring Sister Alacoque to her at once.

Margaret could hardly stand up. The two nuns, much annoyed, almost had to carry her to Mother Saumaise. Margaret sank to her knees and waited for that outraged lady to speak.

"Sister Alacoque! I have tried to be patient with you! But I cannot allow this kind of behavior to go on any longer! Perhaps there is something about all this that I do not understand. Have *you* any explanation? Can *you* tell me why you put on this disgusting display?"

Margaret was still so full of the vision that she could barely speak. Stumbling, stuttering, breaking off in the middle of sentences, she tried to describe what she had seen. Mother Saumaise bit her lip in an effort to keep back the words she would like to have said. "You had better go lie down and rest yourself, Sister," she said instead. "As for these extraordinary permissions you seem to be asking—the answer is no! You will *not* receive Communion on the first Friday of the

month. Visitation nuns receive Communion on
Thursdays and Sundays. And you will *not* get
up to pray for an extra hour on Thursday nights.
The hours of prayer are clearly stated in the rule.
Until you can learn to keep the rule as it is, Sister
Alacoque, I suggest that you do not attempt to
add anything new to it. You may go now!"

When she was alone, Mother Saumaise wrung
her hands. She even allowed herself the consolation of a few tears. She said half aloud, "This
business must be settled—one way or another."
She wiped her eyes, seized a fresh quill and a
piece of paper, and began to write.

"Most Reverend and Dear Father, May I take
the liberty of asking your assistance in a rather
difficult and delicate matter that has arisen in our
monastery. . . ."

One day several weeks later, Margaret was in
the kitchen, warming the plates for her little girls'
dinner. Sister Madeleine des Escures came in,
slightly out of breath, and said sternly, "Go to
the door of the parlor at once, Sister Alacoque.
Our Mother is waiting for you." She added more
kindly, "Are you feeling much better, Sister?"

"Oh yes, thank you, Sister!" Margaret answered. "Completely!"

For weeks after the last vision Margaret had

been desperately ill with a fever that defied the skill of Dr. Billet, the convent physician. As she walked to the parlor, Margaret thought again of how the illness had ended. Perhaps because He knew that His own presence would be too much for the sick girl to bear, Our Lord had sent His mother to her instead.

"Take courage, my dear daughter," the Blessed Mother had said, "in the health that I am giving you in the name of my Divine Son, for you have a long and painful road ahead of you, always in the shadow of the cross. . . . But fear nothing! I will not abandon you and I promise you my protection." She had disappeared then, and so had Margaret's fever and weakness.

Mother Saumaise was waiting at the door of the parlor, looking rather nervous. Margaret too felt nervous. Had she done something wrong again? "Now, Sister," the superior said briskly, "I want you to go into the parlor and talk with the three priests who are waiting for you. Don't look so alarmed, my dear. They are persons of great merit and I'm sure they will help you. Well, don't just stand there, Sister! Go in! They won't eat you."

Margaret went in. The superior closed the door behind her. She would never forget the stricken look on the girl's face. Perhaps she had made a terrible mistake. But what else was there to do?

If she had been walking into a den of hungry lions, Margaret would have gone far more willingly than she now walked into the parlor. Nothing in her life had ever been so painful as this ghastly half hour with the three priests. She could hear her voice stammering out answers to their questions. But her voice seemed to be somebody else's, coming to her from a long distance away. She could not make it say what she wanted it to say.

How could she describe the indescribable? Yes, she had seen the Heart of Jesus—the real Heart of flesh, outside of His Body. Yes, He had asked her to go to Communion as often as she was allowed to do so, and especially on the first Friday of each month. Yes, she knew that going to Communion so often was unusual, but that was what He had said. . . . Yes, she almost continuously heard the voice of God speaking in her heart. No, she had never had a very strong imagination. Yes, it did *seem* as though she must have a strong imagination, but—

And on and on.

Who were these three "persons of merit" who interviewed Margaret? We do not know. One of them was probably a high ranking monk from the neighboring Benedictine abbey. One of them was probably the superior of the Jesuit college in the next block. Whoever they were, their decision was unanimous. They dismissed Margaret and sent for Mother Saumaise. Sister Alacoque, they told her, was no doubt sincere. But her so-called revelations were certainly in her own mind. The less attention that was paid to them, the sooner they would go away. As they were leaving the whitewashed parlor, one of the three men turned back to the grille with a final burst of inspiration.

"Make your Sister Alacoque eat more vegetable soup!" he boomed at Mother Saumaise. "*That* will cure her of her ecstasies!"

Mother Saumaise was now in deeper confusion than she had been before. As for Margaret, the memory of that session in the parlor was a torment for years. Not that she had ever tried to escape suffering. On the contrary. She sought it out. But she was faced with a very real problem, above and beyond the humiliating fact that everyone thought she was slightly mad. Our Lord had given her a mission to accomplish. He had, for some reason, made her a part of His divine plans. There were definite things to be done—things that she was somehow supposed to arrange. But how could *she*, of all people, do anything about it? Her own superior did not believe her. Three learned priests had clearly stated that her heaven-sent mission was a case of nerves, probably caused by lack of vegetables.

Alone before the Blessed Sacrament she poured out her heart to her Beloved. How could she serve His great designs? When would He show her what to do?

One day at last the answer came to her. "*I will send you My faithful servant and perfect friend who will teach you to know Me and to abandon yourself to Me without any more resistance!*"

Here at last was a hope to which she could cling. "My faithful servant and perfect friend!" What a way to be described by God! But who was he? And how would she know him when he came?

FIVE • "BEHOLD THIS HEART—"

"Here she comes! That's her coach!"

The four perfectly matched horses of Monsieur de Lyonne, military governor of the town, swept up the driveway and stopped before the brilliantly-lit house of the mayor.

A crowd of curious townsfolk had gathered to watch the arrival of the guests. As the footman leaped down from the box and opened the door of the governor's coach, the people moved in closer, craning their necks for a better view. A young man gave a timid cheer and the good-natured crowd took it up.

Mademoiselle Marie Rosalie de Lyonne descended from the coach after her mother and entered the house on the arm of her brother, the handsome governor. She was smiling a little at the sound of the friendly cheers. The magnificent Marie Rosalie just naturally had this effect on people.

Inside the house, the mayor's wife nervously fidgeted with her earrings and prepared to welcome her three elegant guests. She was always a little nervous when the de Lyonne ladies were around. "I'm sure they think they're doing me a favor when they come to my parties!" she thought.

"You look just lovely, as always, my dear!" she cooed to Marie Rosalie. "What a stunning gown! It must have come straight from Paris!"

Marie Rosalie glanced absent-mindedly at her pearl-embroidered satin ball dress as though she had forgotten exactly what it was she was wearing. She went into the drawing room and was immediately surrounded by a flock of young men. Most of them had come to the mayor's party only because she had promised to be there.

The mayor's wife sighed and turned to Madame de Lyonne. "I can well understand why Mademoiselle de Lyonne has not married. With so many perfectly charming young men at her feet, *how* could the dear girl make up her mind?"

Madame de Lyonne smiled frostily and went into the drawing room with her son. The innocent remark had touched a sore point. Marie Rosalie did indeed find it hard to choose, although young men from the first families of the country had courted her for years. Of course, the mother thought, no young man who ever lived was good enough for her beautiful Marie Rosalie. But if only she would choose one of them and settle down!

A dark fear haunted the mother's heart. She could not forget that when Marie Rosalie had been a little girl she had once walked past the Visitation convent with her grandmother and had said quite unexpectedly, "What a beautiful house! I shall die in there." Madame de Lyonne had been telling herself for years that this remark was the aimless chatter of a child, but it still weighed on her mind. To be sure, Marie Rosalie, devout as she was, made it clear that the mere thought of entering the convent filled her with horror.

The mayor's party was, as usual, dull and overcrowded. The room quickly became stuffy and the too-sweet ices melted faster than one could eat them. Marie Rosalie yawned behind her fan and wondered how early she and her mother could leave without being rude. The chatter of her young men bored her more than ever to-night. She was glad when she saw Father Forest of the Jesuit college making his way through the crowd. He had just returned from Lyons.

"Ah, good evening, *mon père*," Marie Rosalie said. "What a pleasure to see you! Do sit down and tell us all the news from Lyons."

The young men grudgingly made room for the Jesuit. "There *is* news, Mademoiselle," Father Forest said eagerly. "Great news not only for our college but for the whole town!"

"But how exciting! What *is* it?"

"A new superior has been assigned to our house!"

One of the gentlemen coughed delicately into his handkerchief to hide a laugh. "Earth-shattering!" he whispered to his neighbor.

Marie Rosalie gave him a sharp look, but the Jesuit smiled. "In this case, Monsieur, it is at least surprising. Here we are, one of the smallest and least important houses in the whole Society of Jesus. And for our new superior we are assigned one of the most brilliant men in the whole of France. His name is Claude de la Colombière. He is young but he is already famous as a preacher. He was in Paris for four years and served as tutor to the sons of Monsieur Colbert."

Eyebrows were raised. Anyone who had been in the household of the king's powerful minister of finance must know his way around the court.

"Yet my friends tell me that every spare moment he had was devoted to the poor in the Paris hospitals," the Jesuit went on. "Every Thursday afternoon he tended the sick old people of the home for the aged. And every Sunday morning, the ladies and gentlemen of the court flocked to hear him preach! Do you know what a member of the French Academy said after hearing him? He said, 'He is one of the men of the kingdom who best understand our language.'"

"And such a man has been ordered to *this* place?" said the young man who had laughed. "Why?"

The Jesuit shrugged. "Who knows why superiors do the things they do? And who knows why God Himself does the things that He does? Perhaps there is a good reason why. Perhaps some soul is at this moment in need of just such a man. Perhaps—but what is the matter, Mademoiselle? Are you ill?"

The girl had suddenly turned pale and dropped her fan. "No—no—I feel faint from the heat,

that is all." She hastily excused herself and went
out onto the balcony. The priest's words had
stirred her heart profoundly. In addition to natural goodness, there was a great deal of pride in
that heart. Within a moment she had convinced
herself that the new Jesuit superior was being
sent to Paray-le-Monial for the sole purpose of
solving the problems of Marie Rosalie de Lyonne.

Claude de la Colombière arrived at his new
post early in February of 1675. He was thirty-
four years old. A few days before, he had taken
his final vows as a member of the Society of
Jesus. (This ceremony, then as now, takes place
several years after a Jesuit is ordained a priest.)
He spent the first few days getting the affairs of
his new household in order. Later in the week
he set out to make the expected courtesy calls
on the superiors of the neighboring religious
houses.

The Visitation convent was just around the
corner from the Jesuit house, midway between
it and the Benedictine abbey. Father de la Colombière and Mother Saumaise made a strong and
very good impression on each other through the
parlor grille. "What an excellent young man,"
thought the nun. "So truly spiritual—yet such
perfect manners. One can tell he has just come

from Paris. And *what* a speaking voice! It will
be a rare treat for the sisters to hear him preach."
Out loud she said, *"Mon père*, I know how busy
you are during your first days, but would you
do us the honor of preaching for us soon?"

"The honor would be mine, *ma mère*," said
the Jesuit, and the date of the conference was set
for the following week.

Over eight months had passed since Margaret
had heard those electrifying words, "I will send
you my faithful servant and perfect friend."
They had not been easy months. More than once
she had tried to convince herself that the three
priests in the parlor had been quite right in telling her that the voice she heard was all her
imagination. And if the voice was all imagination, then the promise to send this "faithful
servant" was also only imagination, and he would
never really come.

When word spread through the community
room that the new Jesuit superior was going to
give the nuns a sermon that afternoon, Margaret
paid very little attention. She was, as usual, completely lost in her own thoughts.

The bell rang. The sisters left the community
room and filed into the chapel. The curtain was
drawn back and the young priest on the altar

step began to speak. Margaret did not hear his opening words. Another voice was speaking to her.

"This is he whom I send you!"

Margaret looked up quickly at the Jesuit. For less than a second she studied the pale, slender face, with its dark hair and eyes, and fine, aristocratic nose. Then she lowered her eyes.

For that same fraction of a second, Père Claude hesitated slightly in the middle of a sentence. He was almost unable to follow his train of thought. The light in the nuns' chapel was dim—so dim that he could see nothing but a line of blurred white faces under dark veils. But suddenly in the darkness he saw a face, its great dark eyes looking straight at him. He saw it as clearly as though he were standing in noon sunlight, and he had never before been so moved by the sight of any face.

The conference ended. The nuns left the chapel and Father Claude was conducted to the parlor. Mother Saumaise was beaming from ear to ear. "Ah, *mon père*, I cannot begin to express our appreciation for such a truly—"

"*Ma mère*," the priest said, "Who is that young nun who sits in the last row on the fourth stall from the right?"

If he had interrupted her to ask how much

money was in the convent treasury, Mother
Saumaise would not have been more amazed. But
she said without any sign of surprise, "The fourth
from the right—let me see—that would be—"
She stopped and blinked. "Why—that is Sister
Margaret Mary Alacoque. She—"

"She is a chosen soul," said the priest, then
bowed and left the room abruptly.

Mother Saumaise looked after him, startled.
And then a glimmer of hope was born in her
heart. Margaret was not the only one in the convent who had been praying for help.

Next day Mother Saumaise announced that the
Jesuit superior would act as confessor to the convent during the March ember days. As Margaret
knelt in the chapel, waiting her turn in the confessional, she felt as though the beating of her
heart would suffocate her. This was he who had
been sent. Yet the thought of telling him the
whole story was more than she could bear. The
memory of her forced interview with the three
"persons of merit" was still fresh in her mind.

As he sat in the pitch-dark confessional, Claude
de la Colombière was waiting. All afternoon, all
through the long procession of nuns, from the
superior down, he had been waiting. But waiting
for what? He did not know. Who *was* this Sister
Alacoque with the sad eyes? And why had he so

suddenly become convinced that he had been sent
to Paray-le-Monial on her account? This kind
of experience was new to him. He had never once
in his life had any kind of mystical experience.
Revelations, visions, ecstasies, even the more ordi-
nary kind of spiritual happiness—these things
were unknown to him. He had reached a state
of such holiness that Our Lord Himself considered him "a perfect friend." But he had fought
his way to this state of perfection by a lonely
road. He had been armed only with faith, with
a powerful intellect, and with a dry, unconsol-
ing kind of reason.

When Margaret entered and knelt on the other
side of the screen, Père Claude felt as though the
atmosphere of the totally dark confessional had
suddenly become charged with electricity. Before a word had been spoken, he knew that it
was she.

Faced with the critical moment, however,
Margaret froze. In her low-pitched voice, she
recited her small list of imagined faults, and nothing more. Gently the priest tried to draw something more from her. She realized, then, that
somehow he knew her as she knew him—"for
without our having either seen each other or
spoken, he kept me for a very long time and spoke
as if he understood what was going on inside of

me. But I did not want to open my heart to him at all this time. And when he saw that I wished to leave, for fear of inconveniencing the community, he said to me that if I agreed he would come another time to speak to me in this same place. But my timid nature, fearing these communications, made me answer that this was not up to me and that I would do whatever obedience ordered me to do. I left after having remained about an hour and a half."

Outside the confessional, many of the older nuns were seething with annoyance. Oh, that stupid girl! This was really too much! She was making a fool out of the whole convent in front of a distinguished visitor. To keep the good father trapped for an hour and a half in the confessional with her foolish prattle! They would never have believed that it was actually the good father who was keeping poor Sister Alacoque trapped for an hour and a half. When she finally escaped, she was greeted by the coldest stares and most outraged mutters she had yet seen or heard in the convent.

Père Claude left the convent deeply discouraged. He could not force his help on the nun unless she wanted it. But he knew beyond a shadow of doubt that she needed it. The next day he left town to give a series of missions in the neighboring churches. He did not return to the

Visitation convent until a few weeks after Easter. What took him there was an urgent message from Mother Saumaise. Would Father de la Colombière come around and see her as soon as it was convenient?

He hurried over at once, full of hope. Mother Saumaise met him in the parlor and came to the point at once. "*Mon père*," she said, "I need your help on a most important—and puzzling—matter. You yourself asked me about Sister Alacoque. I would like to tell you about her." And she gave him a brief description of Sister Alacoque's four troubled years in the convent.

"The priests who spoke with her seemed convinced that the girl is imagining all this," she finished. "But frankly, I am not so sure."

He nodded. "And how can I help you, *ma mère*?"

"If I were to send Sister Alacoque to the confessional, would you talk to her?"

"I would be happy to talk to Sister Alacoque," he said.

When Margaret received word that she was to go to the confessional at once and talk with Father de la Colombière, she was half relieved and half frightened. Clearly the time had come when she *must* speak out. But where would she find the words?

"If you knew," she blurted out to him, "how terribly much I dread having to speak to you!"

He thought this over for a few seconds and then gave the one answer that Margaret, being Margaret, could not possibly get around. He said, smiling in the darkness, "But, *ma soeur*, how happy I am to give you the opportunity of making such a sacrifice for God!"

This was the end of Margaret's resistance. Once she had begun to talk, the words came without effort. She told him about her girlhood at L'Hautecour and about the vow she had made during her illness. She told him about the struggles she had gone through to get into the convent and the more difficult struggle she had gone through to stay in it. She told him, too, of her haunting fear that the voice she heard might sometimes be a trap of the devil.

For the first time in her life, Margaret had the benefit of some real, practical direction from a man both intelligent and spiritual enough to understand what this was all about. One by one he solved all her fears. She could not keep her mind on the recited prayers and the scheduled meditations of the convent? Very well, then, he told her. She should say the prayers absolutely required by the Divine Office and not try to say any others. She should meditate however she liked and stop worrying about it.

As to the origin of the voice that spoke to her heart, there was one sure test, he said. Did this mysterious voice ever try to make her do anything that went against religious obedience? No? Then how could it be the voice of the devil who so delights in disobedience to religious superiors?

At last, after several interviews, Margaret told him what she had not yet found the words to tell: the visions of the Sacred Heart and the requests that Our Lord had made to her.

Father Claude then knew that there was more to the strange story than he had at first realized. He was dealing with much more than the problems of a single soul. All the graces and spiritual wonders that this nun had known since her childhood had been given to her for a purpose: to reveal to the world a new devotion to the Sacred Heart of Jesus.

Now devotion to the Sacred Heart was by no means a completely new idea. Claude de la Colombière knew more about its history than Margaret did. Two great saints of the Middle Ages, St. Lutgarde and St. Gertrude, had seen visions of the Heart of Christ. And Father Claude remembered that St. Gertrude, some four hun-

dred years before, had seen a great vision of the
Sacred Heart on the same day as Margaret's first
revelation: the feast of St. John the Evangelist.

Through the years certain saints had known
and practiced the devotion: St. Catherine of Siena;
St. Peter Canisius, a fellow Jesuit; St. John Eudes;
St. Francis de Sales, founder of the Visitation.
There had been others, too. But Père Claude realized that until now this devotion had been understood and loved only by the spiritually great.
Now, it seemed, Our Lord wished to pour the
riches of His Heart on the entire world, on sin-
ners as well as saints. To accomplish this He had
chosen the humble Visitation nun, Margaret
Mary Alacoque. But something more was needed.
Claude de la Colombière realized, with a shock,
that the whole matter now rested on his shoulders.
It was now up to him to apply the tests of reason
and learning to the fiery transports of love that
were granted to Sister Alacoque.

Was there anything in what she said that was
in any way contrary to reason or to the teaching
of the Church? There was not. The burning
Heart of Christ was a symbol. The human heart
has always been a symbol of love. The Sacred
Heart of Jesus, then, was a symbol of divine love,
the flaming love of God for man. This love had

led Him to the supreme moment of human history: the Incarnation. Devotion to the Sacred Heart of Jesus, then, was simply a return of love for love. And when, in the whole long history of the Church, had there been more need for such an expression of love?

What about Sister Alacoque herself? Father Claude proceeded with caution. He put her to every test he could think of. He tried treating her coldly, brushing off her story, catching her in some contradiction. Nothing could shake either her story or her humility. He ended with not a trace of doubt left in his mind.

"You need not fear any longer about Sister Alacoque," he told Mother Saumaise. "The spirit that directs her is truly the voice of God. Everything that she says is true. Let her go her own way. We must simply wait and see what happens next."

One day when Father Claude came to say Mass at the Visitation chapel, another vision came to Sister Alacoque, as she was approaching the Communion rail. "Our Lord . . . showed me His Sacred Heart, like a burning furnace, and two other hearts which joined together and hid themselves in It, saying: *'It is thus that My pure love unites these three hearts forever!'*"

"We must simply wait and see what happens next," the Jesuit had told the superior. What happened next was the supreme moment in the history of devotion to the Sacred Heart. It happened on a day during the octave of Corpus Christi. Margaret, kneeling before the Blessed Sacrament, felt suddenly overcome by the knowledge of God's love for her. She begged Our Lord to tell her how she could possibly make some return to match it.

Instantly He stood before her and said, "You cannot make Me a greater return of love than by doing what I have so many times asked you!"

He showed her His Sacred Heart.

"Behold this Heart," He said, "Which has so loved men that It has spared nothing, even to consuming Itself to witness Its love! And in return, I receive from most of them only ingratitude, from their irreverences and their sacrileges and by the coldness and contempt that they have for Me in this Sacrament of love. . . . Therefore, I ask you that the first Friday after the octave of Corpus Christi be dedicated as a special feast to honor My Heart, that the faithful receive Communion on that day, making reparation to It by a solemn act of amendment for the indignities It has received while exposed on the altars.

"I promise also that My Heart will open to

wield abundantly the influence of Its divine love on those who do it this honor. . . ."

"But, my Lord!" cried Margaret, stunned by the huge request, "to whom are you speaking? To a creature so cowardly . . . that her unworthiness might even prevent the accomplishment of Your design. . . ."

"Ah, poor innocent," He replied. "Don't you know that I use the weak to confound the strong. . . ."

"Give me, then, the means of doing what You order me to do!"

"Address yourself to my servant, Father de la Colombière, and tell him to do all that he possibly can to establish this devotion and give this joy to My Divine Heart. Tell him not to be discouraged by the difficulties that he will meet— and they will not be lacking. But he must know that a man is all powerful when he mistrusts himself completely to trust entirely in Me."

Father Claude ordered Margaret to write down every detail of this great revelation. As he compared it with her account of the first two, he saw before him a kind of blueprint of God's design. The devotion consisted in honoring the human Heart of Christ as the source of His divine love. How could mankind possibly respond to that love? By frequent Communion, particularly on the first Friday of the month; by the holy hour in honor of the Passion; by a special feast in the liturgical calendar on which the entire Church on earth would join together in making reparation to the Sacred Heart of Jesus.

The Jesuit also realized that he, too, had a mission in life beyond anything he had ever dreamed of. The Sacred Heart of Jesus now had two apostles. These two, as best they could, immediately carried out His request. The Friday after the octave of Corpus Christi was June 21st. On that day, each in his own chapel, they solemnly consecrated themselves to the Sacred Heart and vowed to devote their lives to extending Its reign over the whole world.

Thus, although only two people on two city blocks knew it, the first feast of the Sacred Heart was celebrated.

SIX • THE FAITHFUL SERVANT

"But imagine, a man of such learning being taken in by a silly nun!"

"Yes, isn't it odd? Let me tell you what *I* heard! It would be funny if it weren't so annoying!"

Bees droned lazily in the pleasant August afternoon. The voices of the ladies droned louder. The picnic by the river was a great success. All the best young people of the town were invited, and there was plenty of new gossip to be discussed.

Marie Rosalie de Lyonne and her brother had even hired a troupe of wandering gypsy dancers to entertain the guests. Marie Rosalie sat on a pillow, surrounded by her faithful swains. She was not in her usual gay spirits. During the last few months, her friends had noticed, she had often seemed absent-minded and a little sad. And now, while everyone else chattered at once, she sat looking out over the river, lost in her own thoughts.

A third lady said, "You know what Maman heard? Her aunt is a nun at the Visitation, you know. Father Claude actually spent two hours with this girl in the confessional last week. And the next day he was back in the parlor talking to her for an hour! My great-aunt says it's a disgrace that the superior allows her to impose upon him, just because he's kindhearted!"

"Kindhearted and softheaded!" laughed one of the young men. "He's as much a dreamer as the little nun. What's her name again?"

"Alacoque. Sister Margaret Mary Alacoque."

At the sound of the name Marie Rosalie de Lyonne came out of her daydream with a jerk of the head that almost knocked off her floppy straw hat.

"Well, Sister de Sirot—she's a cousin of the Comte de Noailles—says that Father de la Colombière is so taken in by this little fraud that he even has her write down the things she *thinks* she sees and—"

"*What* are you clucking about?" Marie Rosalie interrupted, her eyes flashing.

"About the nun at the Visitation who hears voices," said the young man, lazily shooing flies away from Marie Rosalie with her fan. "I hear—"

"*You* hear!" said Marie Rosalie, angrily snatching her fan out of his hand. "I knew that you loved nothing better than the gossip of stable boys and valets. I *didn't* know that you also collected gossip from convent parlors! What a change for you!"

In the distance a bell rang and Marie Rosalie jumped up. "What time is it?"

"Three o'clock. Why?"

"That's the bell of the Ursuline chapel. Father de la Colombière is preaching there this afternoon. *I'm* going to hear him."

"But, Marie Rosalie," wailed one of the girls. "We haven't even seen the gypsy dancers yet!"

"I'm *going!*" she repeated, straightening her hat. "It would be much better for us to go hear him preach than to sit around amusing ourselves." She looked at the young man coolly. "And talk-

ing about things we don't know anything about!"
With that she swept over the field toward the
little Ursuline chapel. In the end the whole party
trooped after her.

For Marie Rosalie de Lyonne this 28th of
August was a never-to-be-forgotten day. It was
the feast of St. Augustine. "Too late have I loved
thee, O beauty ever old and ever new!" said
Father de la Colombière. He was speaking of
those who resist God's grace for a long time and
then at last give in to it. The great saint's words
echoed again and again in the heart of Marie
Rosalie. When she left the chapel she was a troubled young lady indeed.

The gossip that had amused the picnic party
was being discussed all over town. Père Claude
knew very well that although the people of Paray
liked him, they were secretly laughing at him.
Once, he knew, his pride would have been cut to
the quick by such knowledge. But "Perfection,"
he wrote, "consists in pleasing God. One must
not hesitate over the occasions when one can
please Him, though displeasing men." He ignored
the gossip and laughter as though unaware of its
existence.

And so Margaret entered upon a year of such
peace as she had never known. With her mind

relieved of all doubts, her soul gave itself completely to the graces that God poured into it.

It seems strange to say that a soul already so great now grew even closer to perfection. But that is what happened. Worse trials than she had ever known were still ahead of her. When they came, she would meet them as she had always done. But now she was allowed a little rest.

To Mother Saumaise, too, this year was one of great joy. She and Father Claude had become firm friends. He was her spiritual director and she followed his example by ignoring the sneers of the nuns. Not all the sisters in the convent, of course, made it their business to gossip about Margaret. But to some few of them it seemed scandalous that Sister Alacoque was allowed to receive Communion on an extra day a month and to pray for an extra hour on Thursday nights. They did not know why these days meant anything special to her, or why the superior allowed this tinkering with the rule. But they knew very definitely that they did not like it.

The year and a half of Père Claude's stay in Paray-le-Monial may have been a time of great peace for Margaret, but for Marie Rosalie it was exactly the opposite. Père Claude, the great director of souls, recognized the truth that the girl hid so well from herself: she was fighting a losing

battle against a religious vocation. Marie Rosalie
denied this. She did *not* want to enter a convent,
she kept telling herself and the priest. She was
quite content to say her prayers and to do good
works, like organizing Père Claude's campaign
to build a decent hospital in town. Eventually,
she would meet some young nobleman with more
brains than the ones she knew, and get married.

Père Claude thought otherwise. But he was determined to make her work it out for herself.
"As soon as one has learned how great and lovable Our Lord is," he told her, "one loves Him
dearly and never thinks one can do enough for
Him."

Marie Rosalie had at least one good excuse and
she kept bringing it up. "Of course my mother
would *never* allow me to enter a convent!"

"Your mother would be only too happy if
you would make up your mind to marry one of
the young counts and even dukes who court you.
Surely she would not stand in the way if you
wished to be the bride of a King!"

"Oh, yes she would, Father!" said Marie Rosalie. "You don't know Maman!"

September of 1676 came. One day Father
Claude received a letter from the provincial. He
was to leave Paray-le-Monial at once, the letter

said, to become superior of a larger school. "It is a kind of death to leave a place where one is well known and has friends," he had once written. Leaving Paray and the friends he had there was the hardest thing he had ever done. But willingness to be sent from one place to another on short notice is part of a Jesuit's life.

He went to the convent to break the news of his departure to Sister Alacoque. As the curtain before the grille was drawn back, he looked at her and thought, "How pale she is!" The recent death of her mother, he knew, had been a sad blow. "*Ma soeur*," he began. "I have something to tell you—"

"You are going away," she said. "I know. And so far away!"

He smiled. "How did you know? I have told no one yet. But it is not so far—only a half day's journey. I shall visit here as often as I can."

"But you are going to England!"

Father Claude was thunderstruck. England! What would he be doing in England? There was as much chance of his going to the moon. "You've been dreaming, Sister," he said. "I am going away—yes. But not to England. What makes you think—?"

The bell rang. It was time for Vespers. Without a word more than a whispered good-by, Mar-

garet hurried out of the parlor. Father Claude
went home, ill at ease. He did not take anything
Sister Alacoque said lightly. But surely this time
she *had* been dreaming.

Some days later, while he was packing his
books, a messenger arrived from the provincial
with a sealed letter. Father Claude de la Colombière, it said, should proceed at once to Paris.
There he would be told the details of a mission
of great secrecy and importance for which he
had been chosen. He was appointed chaplain to
Mary of Modena, the Italian princess who had
married the Duke of York, brother of King
Charles II. After receiving instructions, he was to
leave at once for England.

Charles II had become king of Protestant England fifteen years before. Until then he had spent
nearly all of his life in exile, waiting for the day
when he might be restored to the throne of his
father. The day had finally come in 1661. Among
the restored king's chief problems was the vio-
lent feelings of his people on the matter of religion. Rival Protestant groups fought among
themselves. They had only one thing in common. They all hated the Catholics.

There is little doubt that King Charles himself was secretly convinced that he should be a

Catholic. To admit this, however, would mean losing his throne. And, as he himself put it, after so many years in exile he did not intend to start out on his travels again!

The storm center of religious argument was the king's brother, James. For the Duke of York was openly a Catholic. The trouble was that King Charles had no children who could legally succeed him. This meant that the next in line to the throne was the king's Catholic brother. It was a ticklish situation.

Three years before, James had married the beautiful Italian princess, Mary Beatrice of Modena. The lovely girl had not wanted to go to England to marry a man twenty-five years older than herself. She had not wanted to become either Duchess of York or Queen of England. Her only ambition had been to become a Visitation nun. This she had not been allowed to do.

Among the terms of Mary's marriage contract was the strict agreement that she would be allowed to have her own chaplain and to hear Mass in her own chapel. The post of chaplain to the duchess was a most important one, for the Duke and Duchess of York were close to the king, and whoever served in their household as spiritual adviser might also be able to influence Charles II. There was another important job for the Duchess's chaplain. The chapel of the household was not considered a public place of worship. This meant that it was about the only place in London where Catholics who dared to do so could hear Mass and receive the Sacraments. English priests were forbidden to say Mass anywhere, public or private. Whatever foreign priest, then, served as chaplain to the Duchess of York was practically the only priest in London who could preach openly to English Catholics. The man to fill such a post needed many great gifts: holiness and courage; intelligence and tact; a knowledge of the ways of kings and courts. The French Jesuit superiors, called upon to fill the order, had looked over their ranks and unhesitatingly chosen Claude de la Colombière.

He left for England on October 5, 1676. He had received secret orders from the King of France about converting the King of England. But as he watched the green shores of Normandy disappear behind his ship, he knew that his greatest mission in England would be to spread the joyous message confided to him by the King of Heaven.

"I seek a victim for My Heart! . . . I wish for no one else but thee!"

Five years before, the young novice had heard

these mysterious words. She had gladly accepted the challenge. Toward the end of the year 1677, the challenge loomed up before her in a very real way. On a night filled with terror and mystery she drained the chalice that she had promised to drink. The events of that November 20th have never been fully revealed because in writing about them, Margaret was too charitable to tell the whole story.

For some months the saint had known that God was greatly displeased with certain members of her community. There is no way around the fact that in this convent, blessed with so many saintly nuns, there were a few thoroughly bad ones too. These women, forced by their families into the convent without true vocations, might not have seemed particularly bad out in the world, where they belonged. On a gravel path, one piece of stone looks very much like another and does not attract special notice. But transfer these jagged little stones to a case of diamonds and pearls, and they look very ugly indeed. In the Visitation, one of the truly great religious orders of that day as of this, the unworthiness of these few souls loomed large indeed.

Our Lord had revealed to Margaret that the hand of God's justice was ready to fall heavily

upon these five or six nuns—unless she would
offer herself as a victim to appease the divine
wrath. What He was doing was asking her to
repeat, on a tiny scale, His own sacrifice for the
sins of the whole world. During the Thursday
holy hours He had already let her share His
agony in the garden. Now, in her own way, she
would live through the sorrows of the night that
followed, the night of the trial by his enemies.

Our Lord showed her "all that I would have
to suffer to appease His just anger. . . . I did not
have the courage to sacrifice myself," she adds
sorrowfully. The sacrifice had to be voluntary,
as Christ's had been, and for a long time she
struggled against making it.

Every year on the feast of the Presentation,
the nuns solemnly renewed their vows. On the
eve of the feast Margaret realized that the time
had come when she no longer dared resist the
divine wishes. For she suddenly saw how fiercely
God's just anger was turned against her beloved
convent. There was a terrible price to pay for
her long resistance. Our Lord now told her that
the sacrifice would have to be made publicly,
"accompanied by circumstances so humiliating
that they will be a subject of confusion for the
rest of your life!"

It was nearly six o'clock in the evening. When

the nuns left the chapel for dinner, Margaret stayed behind in the chapel, weeping bitterly. She knew that the moment had finally come. When she tried to follow the others to the refectory, she could hardly walk. "I felt myself burning in a raging fire which reached the very marrow of my bones . . . and I could not say anything except, 'My God! Have pity on me!' "

At about eight o'clock one of the other nuns found her and took her to the superior, who was sick in the infirmary.

"What is it, my child? What has happened?" cried Mother Saumaise, when she saw the tortured, tear-stained face at her bedside.

Barely able to speak, Margaret told her the frightening story: that God demanded the sacrifice of herself, in the presence of the community, and why.

Mother Saumaise shuddered. She knew what the girl would bring on herself by such an act. But she also knew that for Margaret there was no turning back. "Go my child, and do what you must do," she said. "And God be with you!"

It was now nearly 8:30. The nuns were getting ready to go to the chapel for Matins when Margaret came into the community room, walked to the middle of the floor and sank to her knees.

Sister Alacoque's strange behavior in chapel and absence from the evening meeting had already been noted. Now here she was on her knees, with her eyes red and her face splotchy. Eyebrows were raised and sharp looks exchanged.

Nervously the assistant superior asked the usual question for closing the evening: did anyone have anything further to say?

For a moment nobody spoke, and then the unbelievable happened.

Sister Alacoque began to speak. She had been ordered by God to offer herself as a victim of reparation for the sins of her beloved sisters, she began, for their sins against the rule, for their lack of charity, humility, obedience. . . .

When Margaret had finished what she had to say, there was a moment of terrible silence in the room, and then the storm broke. What Margaret had done was certainly contrary to every known rule of well-ordered convent life. First, she had accused some of her sisters of unworthiness and of laxness in keeping the rule by which they all lived. Since no one as yet knew that God Himself had revealed all this to her, it seemed to the sisters that she had passed this harsh judgment on her own authority. Yet *she* was the one who had nearly been sent home because of her inability to keep the rule! *She* was the one who had made the convent the laughingstock of the town!

To make matters worse, she had then claimed that she, of all people, could somehow expiate the sins of the whole community by offering herself as a victim! All of the nuns, even her friends, were not a little shocked by this unusual scene, and naturally the five or six people for whom she had made this horrible sacrifice were the most outraged of all, since they were the only ones with guilty consciences.

When the bell rang for the beginning of the night's silence, Margaret escaped from the community room and rushed back to the infirmary, to the one place of refuge she had. Matins over, the bell rang for bed time. Margaret looked hopefully at Sister Marest. If only she would let her stay by the bedside of Mother Saumaise, she would be safe! But Sister Marest, troubled by the strange goings-on that she did not understand, hurried her out the door.

As Margaret stepped out into the dark corridor, she found five or six of the nuns waiting for her, blocking her way to her cell. She did not reach it that night.

Nobody knows what really happened during those bleak hours until dawn. Margaret says only this: "I am certain that I have never suffered so

much, not even if I could gather up all the sufferings that I had known up to then, and all those
that I have known since, and if all these together should last continually up to my death, all
this would not seem comparable to what I endured that night. . . . The night having passed
in what torments God knows, and without rest,
towards the hour of Mass, it seemed to me that
I heard these words: 'At last peace is made and
My holy justice is satisfied by the sacrifice that
you have made for Me. . . . For in imitation of
Me, you have suffered this in silence, with no
other interest but the glory of God in establishing the reign of My Sacred Heart in those of
men. . . .''

People who would like to write history without recording the evil as well as the good are
well-meaning but misguided, for they forget
that *all* things work for the glory of God. So,
in spite of themselves, did Margaret's enemies,
for by means of them the saint had shared in
the night of Christ's passion. The depths of suffering to which she had sunk on that night only
make her ultimate triumph more glorious.

When Mother Saumaise wrote Father de la
Colombière about that sad night, he replied: "If
I did not believe that God would yet have mercy

on those good women I should be all but inconsolable. How despairing if, while Our Lord blesses the work here, the enemy of our salvation destroys elsewhere what I was so happy to have strengthened by the grace of God."

An old Portuguese proverb says, "God writes straight with crooked lines." At Paray-le-Monial Margaret now lived under a cloud of suspicion and ill-will. The convent recovered very slowly from the memory of that dreadful night. To some members of the community it seemed that only one explanation was possible. Sister Alacoque was possessed by the devil. Many of them took to dousing her with holy water and muttering prayers whenever she passed. Margaret was very much hurt by this until the day Our Lord whispered to her, "But I *love* holy water . . . !"

For the time being, then, there was no question of Margaret's doing anything to advance the great work to which she had consecrated her life. She simply kept quiet and waited for God to work things out in His own good time. This He was already doing.

While Margaret prayed in silence, Claude de la Colombière preached aloud. Thus it happened that the heart-warming message of the Sacred Heart of Jesus was first told to the Catholics of

England, during the darkest days of their lives.

Only four months after his arrival, Father Claude was writing these words in his notebook: "I realized that God wished me to serve Him in procuring . . . devotion to the Sacred Heart. This was revealed by Him to a person with whom He communicates intimately and through whom He was pleased to make use of my weakness. She explained all this to me. . . . I have already inspired this [devotion] to many people in England."

He moved slowly in speaking publicly of the Sacred Heart, for his very first mention of it met with a storm of protest from some English priests who, like so many others, were under the influence of Jansenism. But on the feast of Corpus Christi, he spoke out openly and said at the end of his sermon: "Oh, my God, give us a new heart, a tender, sensitive heart, not one of marble or bronze. Give us a heart like Yours. Give us Your own Heart. Come, lovable Heart of Jesus, into my breast. Light there a love capable, if it were possible, of fulfilling my duty to love my Saviour. Adorable Heart, let me love this divine Saviour as He loves me. Let me from now on love only in and for Him that I may live with Him forever in heaven!"

On the Friday after the octave of Corpus

Christi, Father Claude renewed his consecration to the Sacred Heart, knowing that Sister Alacoque was doing the same thing in Paray. The weary distance between France and England seemed shorter to him that day.

Père Claude's stay in England was drawing to a close more quickly than he knew. He already realized that he was surrounded by spies and secret enemies. He was a Frenchman and he was a Jesuit. To an English Protestant this was the worst thing that could be said about anyone. Ill health added to his danger. He had never been strong, and the cold, damp English climate was too much for his lungs. He began to spit blood. Soon he was so weak that he could "neither write, nor speak—hardly pray."

And now the tables were turned on Père Claude. Once he had been a tower of strength to a confused and unhappy little nun. Now it was she who supported him through his days of trial. After Margaret's death, Mother Saumaise wrote this about her and Father Claude. "Our Lord showed her one day the crosses and spiritual sufferings which he endured in the country to which his superiors sent him. She came to tell me of this and to give me a note for him which contained great consolation dictated by Jesus Christ Himself. Soon after, I received a letter from this great servant of God and knew by what he asked that he had great need of prayers. . . . Père de la Colombière received the note and told me that it had come in the nick of time and that he did not know what he would have done without it."

Margaret's letters were few. He received news of her through Mother Saumaise, whose warm friendship he valued so much. "I cannot tell you," he wrote her one day, "what a consolation your letter was to me. The note from Sister Alacoque strengthens me greatly and reassures me over the thousand doubts which assail me every day. . . ."

Toward the end of 1678, a scoundrel named Titus Oates produced some clumsily forged "evidence" that the English Catholics were planning to kill the king and place the Duke of York on the throne. From the king down, no one in authority really believed Oates's confused lies. But among the Catholic-hating mob, such accusations were a favorite pasttime. Catholics in general, and Jesuits in particular, had been accused of everything from the great fire of London to the epidemic of plague. Oates's clumsy story seemed a fine excuse to go out hunting Catholics. A band of English Jesuits—soon to be martyrs— were the first to be arrested. Claude, now so weak that he could hardly move, lay alone in his room waiting for the inevitable day when he would join them. One morning there was a knock on his door. The priest struggled to sit up and put on his shoes. This was surely the moment he had been expecting. He opened the door. An old man stood outside, dressed in tattered, ill-fitting clothes. He was a Franciscan friar, he told Père Claude. He did not have much of a disguise, did he? He did not really expect to be alive much longer anyway. "I come," he told Père Claude, "to seek strength and counsel of the Sacred Heart of Jesus of Which you are known far and wide among us as the apostle."

What a wonderful moment it must have been for the sick man! All day long the Jesuit and the future Franciscan martyr talked to each other about this rediscovered treasury of love. Early next morning the old friar said the Mass of All Saints Day at the altar which Claude had dedicated to the Sacred Heart, and then said goodby. They never met again.

On November 24, 1678, Claude de la Colombière was arrested for treason. The charges against him were serious, and, no doubt, absolutely true. They give us a clear picture of the work that he had been doing since his arrival in England. He was accused of having converted a startling num-

ber of Protestants and former Catholics. He was
also charged with the smuggling of priests safely
out of the country, to France and to the Virginia
colony. Contrary to law, he had said Mass and
secretly carried the sacraments all over London.
He had tried to convert the king and had said
out loud that his majesty was already a Catholic
at heart.

He was sent to the filthiest prison in London
to await sentencing. Since any one of the charges
against him was punishable by death, there was
little doubt in his mind about what the sentence
would be.

But while Claude lay ill in prison, waiting to
join the other martyrs, his friends on the outside were working frantically to save his life. In
the end, the fact that he was a hated Frenchman actually saved it. The King of France sent
word to England demanding the release of a
French citizen held without authority in an
English prison. At last Father Claude was sen-
tenced to be banished from England.

On December 31, 1678, he left London to return to France. He had missed martyrdom by a
hairsbreadth. He himself decided that he had
simply been unworthy of such a gift. It is more
likely that he was spared because the most important part of his mission still lay ahead of him.

SEVEN • MOTHER GREYFIÉ AND THE ANGELS

"Put one more bit of fern in it, Sister. Then it will be perfect!" Sister des Escures stood back to admire the bouquet that Sister Marie-Bénigne was arranging.

"But do hurry, Sister dear! I'm sure she will be here at any minute!" said little Sister Anne Rosselin, darting to the window. "I think I hear a coach coming now!"

Once again a new superior was coming to the nuns at Paray-le-Monial. Mother Saumaise's term had run out and she had left for Dijon. The new superior was named Mother Greyfié. Her reputation had come ahead of her.

"Oh, I'm sure we've been blessed to have been sent such a superior!" said Sister des Escures, rolling her eyes to heaven. "They say she's absolutely devoted to the rule and insists on its *strict* observance!"

Sister de Sirot looked up from her embroidery and directed a frosty smile in the direction of Sister Alacoque who was sitting across the room, sewing. "That will certainly make life difficult for *some* people around here. I hope that—"

"She's here! She's here!" called Sister Anne Rosselin from the window. The nuns hurried to the door with their flowers.

Mother Péronne-Rosalie Greyfié was forty-four years old when she came to Paray-le-Monial, in June of 1678. She had been a nun for twenty-seven years and had been brought up at Annecy, in the first Visitation convent. She had even known Mother de Chantal, the founder of the order. Naturally she was devoted to the rule. And naturally she was somewhat startled, upon arriving at her new post, to hear strange stories from the senior nuns about a certain young Sister Alacoque. Particularly alarming were the accounts she heard of the night of November 20th, six months before. That sort of thing, she thought firmly, would never happen again. She would get this Sister Alacoque down to earth and keep her there.

Mother Greyfié was a woman who never minced words. In her first long talk with Margaret she bluntly stated: "My dear Sister, I want you to forget all these things you are saying about establishing devotion to the Sacred Heart. Put it out of your mind. Treat it as the vainest figment of your imagination! When you see these things you *think* you see, or hear these imaginary voices, ignore them! Believe me, child, the sooner you get over these illusions, the better it will be for all of us!"

Later in her life Mother Greyfié would reproach herself for being so harsh to Margaret. Her attitude, however, made sense up to a point. She had no way of knowing whether this Sister Alacoque of hers was a true visionary or a vain, deluded girl. As the new superior put Margaret's humility and obedience to one test after another, she watched her closely, trying to find one little defect that would prove the point and settle her mind. Then slowly, even reluctantly, she was forced to wonder whether Sister Alacoque did not, after all, have some direct communication with heaven.

That incident about the infirmary, for example. . . .

Sister Alacoque's health was most unsatisfactory. She suffered terribly from a mysterious pain in her left side. She was subject to migraine headaches. Bouts of a malarial-type fever constantly kept her in the infirmary. In the summer of 1678 she had been there for nearly a month, so weak that she could hardly walk. But the next day was Corpus Christi. The thought of missing Mass on the feast of the Blessed Sacrament was a cruel disappointment.

When Mother Greyfié came to visit the patients, Margaret begged for permission to get up next morning and hear Mass. "If *you* say it's all right, Mother, Our Lord will say it's all right too and will give me the strength!"

Mother Greyfié was not so sure, but she told Sister Marest to give Margaret some hot food in the morning and to get her up just in time for Mass. That night Margaret felt a little stronger and begged her nurse to let her remain fasting all night and morning so that she could receive Communion. (Until quite recently, the Communion fast had to be kept from midnight.)

"Well, if you feel well enough, why not?"

said the good-natured nun. "I'll tell Mother that I think you can manage, and I'm sure she'll give us permission." But Sister Marest had a busy time and the matter slipped her mind. Next morning, as she was helping Margaret dress, she suddenly exclaimed, "Good heavens! I forgot to get permission for you to fast and receive Communion. I'll go at once and tell Mother that you're perfectly able to. I won't be a minute!"

Half a minute after Sister Marest had gone out one door, Mother Greyfié came in the other door. "Well, Sister," she said briskly, "how are you feeling? Did you have a good hot breakfast? You'll need all your strength to get up, after being in bed so long."

"I feel very much better, Mother," Margaret said, although she was actually exhausted from the mere activity of getting dressed. "But I didn't eat breakfast. I thought perhaps I could fast and receive—"

She would have gone on to say that Sister Marest was even then on her way to arrange this, when Mother Greyfié interrupted her. "You *thought*!" she exploded. "You wouldn't also have *thought* of asking permission, would you? The thought didn't just happen to cross your mind, did it? You certainly have a way of making your own rules, Sister Alacoque." She went on along these lines for some time, until the sick girl's un-intended disobedience sounded like a criminal offense in the first degree.

Margaret could easily have justified herself at the expense of the absent-minded Sister Marest, but she did not say a word. Mother Greyfié, red in the face, said, "All right, Sister, if that's the way you want it, *go* to Mass. *Go* to Communion. You always do exactly what you want to do any-way! But if you're feeling so well, then you're well enough to get out of the infirmary and *stay* out of it! I forbid you to set foot in here for—for—six months!"

A few minutes later as she herself, still fum-ing, was on her way to the chapel, Sister Marest finally caught up with her. "Oh, *ma mère*," she said breathlessly, "I've been looking all over for you! I was supposed to ask you last night. I told Sister Alacoque that she could remain fasting and that I'd get permission. And then it completely slipped my mind. Don't worry about her, though. Poor dear, she's so happy at the thought of go-ing to Communion that it's given her strength. And right after Mass I'll pack her back into bed with a nice cup of hot milk."

The superior gulped. "She won't be coming back." She added weakly, "I have forbidden her to come to the infirmary for six months."

Sister Marest gasped. "She's not coming back? But Mother! She's *sick*!"

"Oh, dear," said Mother Greyfié to herself. "Why don't I *think* a little more before I speak? She can't *possibly* stay well for six months. I shall have to take it back!"

But as the day and the week passed, the superior saw that there was really no need to take it back. Sister Alacoque, who had hardly been able to walk alone, felt all her strength return during the Mass of Corpus Christi. And she found herself in a state of glowing health that she had not known since her childhood.

One day in February a very worried Sister Anne Rosselin brought word to Mother Greyfié that Sister Alacoque had just been taken to the infirmary with a raging fever. She had been seized with it right after Mass and had suddenly become so weak that she could not walk without help.

Mother Greyfié did some quick mental arithmetic and realized, with a strange feeling in her heart, that it was exactly six months to the day since the feast of Corpus Christi. "Sister Alacoque," she thought, almost lightheaded, "loves the virtue of obedience. But she must have had some outside help in obeying me this time!"

Claude de la Colombière was back in Paray, to make a brief visit on his way to the Jesuit college at Lyons. As soon as he could escape from the eager crowd of visitors who wore out the little strength he had, he hurried to the Visitation convent and stood once more in the familiar white parlor.

Less familiar was the sight that greeted him as the grille curtain was pulled back: an unfriendly face. Mother Greyfié introduced herself and greeted him politely but coolly. When he asked whether Sister Alacoque could come to the parlor, the face became even less friendly. No, she was very sorry, but Sister Alacoque could *not* come to the parlor. If the good father wanted to speak with Sister Alacoque for some reason which she could not imagine, then he would have to do so in the confessional. After this ungracious speech she steamed off and sent a messenger to order the sister to the chapel.

How wonderful it would be to have some record of this conversation between the two saints. But there is none. We do know that after their meeting Father Claude wrote this to Mother Saumaise: "Passing through Paray, I was only able to see Sister Alacoque once, but the visit was a great consolation to me. I found her as always extremely humble and obedient, with a great love of the cross and of humiliations. These are the marks of the spirit which leads her and which has never yet deceived anyone!"

Margaret's yearning for the suffering and humiliations that would unite her more and more to her Beloved was amply filled by Mother Greyfié. Of all the abuse that the superior heaped on her, the incident that she later regretted the most came after the reunion of the two apostles of the Sacred Heart. For at the next meeting of the community, Mother Greyfié, who had herself ordered Margaret to go to the confessional, now delivered a tirade against her for having gone and for having stayed too long. "You think yourself so much more interesting than the rest of us, Sister Alacoque," she said in a withering tone. "So naturally you think nothing of embarrassing the whole community for your personal satisfaction!"

Years later Mother Greyfié wrote: "Anyone else but she would have reminded me that she herself had not asked for this interview and had gone to it out of obedience. And she could have said other things too and no one would have blamed her for complaining! . . . But far from this . . . she put it all to the uses of her humility and sweetness and patience and never made the least protest of her innocence."

Word of this public accusation leaked out through the parlor grille and quickly came to the ears of Father Claude. He thought it all over for a few days and finally decided to pay another call on Mother Greyfié before he left town. This time he talked as bluntly to that sharp-tongued lady as she had been talked to for some time.

"You acted wisely in testing Sister Alacoque yourself," he said. "But to continue in this any longer would be rash indeed! Do you really believe that such humility and obedience could survive so long if Sister Alacoque were simply deluded? As to the devil, can you really believe that *he*, of all people, would produce this perfection in any soul? If indeed it *is* the devil who is trying to deceive Sister Alacoque, then believe me, he is only succeeding in deceiving himself! I tell you, *ma mère*, that I have never believed anything more strongly than I believe that Sister Margaret Mary Alacoque is truly a soul chosen by God for a great purpose!"

Mother Greyfié was doubly shaken now, for she herself was already half convinced that what he said was true.

Once again Père Claude had done battle for Margaret. Once again, her confidence in herself, weakened by the obvious distrust of her superior, was happily restored.

And once again, Père Claude, while restoring peace to the troubled soul of one girl, was stirring up a spiritual hornets' nest in the soul of another.

Marie Rosalie de Lyonne was still single and was still turning down good matches, although by the standards of her day, she was getting on in years. As for a religious vocation, she was still toying with the idea as one toys with a very short, lighted match.

During the years of Father Claude's absence, a strange and most unlikely friend had come into Marie Rosalie's life: Sister Alacoque. The two women were about as unlike as any two women could be. The humble, self-effacing nun and the wealthy, self-willed aristocrat had, in the beginning, only one thing in common: their confessor, Father de la Colombière. The two had met in a most unusual way.

Our Lord, knowing that without a shove in the right direction, Marie Rosalie would never give in to her vocation, had asked Margaret to take a hand in the matter. Margaret had written about this to Father Claude in England. He, in turn, had written to Marie Rosalie in Paray and asked her to pay a call on Sister Alacoque, who wanted to see her.

Mademoiselle de Lyonne had answered this roundabout invitation with great reluctance. "What am I *doing* here?" she thought desperately, as she waited in the Visitation parlor. "I just know she'll be dreadful and have awful manners and preach at me and tell me to become a nun! Well, I *won't*!" She pulled her great fur-lined cape up around her neck and shivered.

But when the curtain was drawn back and Sister Alacoque appeared and began to speak, Marie Rosalie was quickly won over by her gentle manner and sweet words. Suddenly she blurted out, "*Ma soeur*, Père de la Colombière told me that you were the saintliest person he had ever known! I'll follow your advice in every way—except about entering a convent! Don't even mention it to me, *please*, dear Sister!"

Sister Alacoque smiled. "But Mademoiselle," she said, "there are so many other things to talk about!"

Thus the odd pair became friends. But Marie Rosalie, with good reason, was still suspicious. One day Margaret sent for her and said, "Would you be good enough to say the thirty-days' prayer for a special intention of mine?"

Marie Rosalie agreed but as she left the parlor

she thought, "Aha! She doesn't fool me! Her special intention is that I'll become a nun! But I'll fool her! *My* intention in saying the prayer will be that I *never* become a nun!"

Clearly Sister Alacoque's intention had more influence than Mademoiselle de Lyonne's. The day the prayer ended Our Lord again told Margaret that He was still waiting patiently for Marie Rosalie. Again Margaret passed this message on to Father Claude. By this time he was back in France, stationed at Lyons. He wrote to Marie Rosalie that he had something important to tell her. When she received the letter, she immediately ordered her horse to be saddled, and with one of her brothers as an escort, she set out at a gallop for Lyons, fifteen miles away.

Her worst fears were realized. "My daughter," the priest said to her, "if Jesus Christ demanded you for His bride, would you refuse Him?"

"*O mon père—!*"

"God wishes it, my daughter! Would you refuse this honor? *Could* you refuse Jesus Christ?"

At these words Marie Rosalie felt her horror at the idea melt away. As she rode home, she felt so uplifted that she kept calling out dramatically, "Farewell, fields! Farewell, little birds! Farewell, brook!"

Her brother galloped behind her, barely able

to match the pace she had set her horse. "For heaven's sake, Marie Rosalie," he shouted at her, "will you keep quiet! What will people think?"

But at that moment Marie Rosalie could not have cared less what anybody thought.

Needless to say, Madame de Lyonne did not share her daughter's spiritual elation. She carried on so pitifully that Marie Rosalie, who loved her mother dearly, lost her nerve. She would drop the whole idea, she told her family.

Or so she thought. One morning, several weeks later, Sister Alacoque approached Mother Greyfié and said, "Mother dear, what shall we do? Our Lord spoke to me again last night about Mademoiselle de Lyonne. He said, 'I want that soul! I want it at any cost—!'"

Mother Greyfié, to her credit, did not argue over the source of this message. She thought about it for a few moments and said, "I have it! We will send a note asking her to come to Mass this morning. We will say that we wish to have a word with her."

Marie Rosalie answered the summons and came to Mass with two of her friends. After Mass the girls went into the parlor and there Mother Greyfié and Sister Alacoque told Marie Rosalie that it was time to act—now! She must simply walk through the convent door that minute, and send a message to her mother after she was in. It was the only way.

Marie Rosalie blanched. "B-but, what will Mother say?" she asked weakly.

"My dear," said Mother Greyfié, rolling her eyes eloquently, "you are thirty-five years old!"

Marie Rosalie took a deep breath. "Very well. I'll do it." She turned to her friends. "Go home and tell my brother. He will tell Mother." She kissed the girls and walked unsteadily toward the rarely opened door that led into the cloister. On the threshold she turned and said dramatically, "I have only one consolation! I won't live more than two weeks here! I *know* I won't."

She died forty-five years later at the age of eighty-one.

Once inside the cloister, Marie Rosalie found that all her fears had been no more real than nightmares. She was ecstatically happy. She did not even mind when her fellow novices teased her by calling her their grandmother. "Very well, little ones," she told them, "will you please help your grandmother with her Latin because she never learned a word of it!"

From her first day in the convent Marie Rosalie's new sisters were completely delighted with her. The charm and the generosity of spirit that had made her so well loved in the world had the same effect in the convent.

Now the aristocratic Marie Rosalie made no bones about the fact that she regarded the humble Sister Alacoque as a living saint upon earth. Several of the nuns who had always felt the greatest contempt for Margaret suddenly began to wonder why the delightful and noble Sister de Lyonne thought so highly of her.

Human nature is human nature—in every country and every century.

Margaret now had a very valuable ally. So, indirectly, did the Sacred Heart.

"Several months ago I received a letter from Sister Alacoque full of the divine Spirit," Father de la Colombière wrote Mother Saumaise. ". . . In regard to myself, she orders me from her dear Master no longer to think of the past, to make no plans for the future and for the present to take charge of an invalid whom Our Lord has confided to my charge to exercise me in charity and patience. She says that this invalid is myself and that I must have no scruples about doing my best to recover. I shall obey blindly."

The invalid was in need of much care. He had never regained his health after his ordeal in England. He felt that he was a terrible burden to the

Society, for he was rapidly reaching the end of his strength. But in many ways the work that he did during the last two years of his life was the most important work of all. Unable to take on a more taxing assignment, he had become spiritual director to the young Jesuit students in the major seminary. To these young men he confided the secret treasures of the Sacred Heart of Jesus. And these future priests, fired with zeal by their great teacher, would soon be leaving the seminary to take up their lives as parish priests, as preachers, as teachers and as missionaries. Wherever they went, to every corner of France and the world, they would carry the message with them. From these beginnings grew the great Jesuit tradition of love for the Sacred Heart, an apostolate that continues to this day.

On Easter of 1681 Père Claude had such a terrible lung hemorrhage that his superiors ordered him out of the foggy city of Lyons at once. For the last time he returned to Paray-le-Monial, the spot closest to his heart. He found the beautiful Marie Rosalie as radiant in her stark black habit as she had ever been in her brocades and diamonds. "Oh, my daughter!" he exclaimed, as her smiling face greeted him through the grille, "what a joy it is to me to see you at last the bride of Christ!"

Marie Rosalie struggled for some words that could tell him how indescribably rich her life had become. "Oh, Father," she said at last, thus saying everything, "how good God is!"

By January of 1682 Father Claude was too weak to leave his room. Dr. Billet ordered him to a warmer climate. Much as he dreaded the trip, the priest yearned to see his brother in the south of France. A carriage was hired and the sick man made quiet preparations to leave town without the necessity of wearing good-bys. But he sent Mademoiselle de Bisefranc, one of his friends and penitents, who was in on the secret, to carry his farewell to Sister Alacoque. To his surprise, the lady came back with the message that he was not to leave Paray unless he was forced to do so because of religious obedience.

Unable to believe that the message was accurate, he sent back a note asking for an explanation. Sister Alacoque took a scrap of paper and wrote on it only these words: "He told me that He desires the sacrifice of your life here!"

Several days later, on February 15th, Claude de la Colombière died of a sudden lung hemorrhage. When Mademoiselle de Bisefranc brought the news of his death to the convent, early in the morning, Margaret said to her sadly, "Pray! And make everyone pray for him!" But a few hours

later she suddenly stopped what she was doing
and wrote a hasty note to the grieving messenger.
"Do not be sad any more. Pray *to* him, now, and
do not be afraid of anything! He is more powerful to help you than he has ever been!"

The death of her dearest friend, the scorn and
distrust of so many of her beloved sisters, the
misery of continual illness, the pain of frequent
accidents—all these things in her life she willingly accepted. They were part of the agreement
made on the day she had offered herself as a victim for the triumph of the Sacred Heart. These
sufferings, offered for such a purpose, were already supernaturalized. And then, on a day when
heaven came close to earth, they were trans-
figured still further. The picture, already a mas-
terpiece, was put in a golden frame.

One day during recreation, as the sisters were
in the garden working at their spinning, Margaret
heard a wordless, irresistible voice calling her.
The voice was urging her to go to the little courtyard, formed by the jutting walls of the chapel,
where she often prayed. She had sought out this
spot many times before during recreation, for she
was often overcome with longing for the Blessed
Sacrament and she knew the exact spot on the
stone wall behind which the tabernacle stood.

She hastily asked the superior's permission to leave the group, then hurried through the garden to the deserted courtyard.

At once she saw why she had been summoned.

In the sky over her head there was a flaming vision of the Sacred Heart of Jesus, surrounded by the indescribably beautiful creatures whom she recognized at once as the Seraphim—the glorious angels who constantly sing the divine praises around the throne of God.

They were singing now, singing their seraphic song that she could never quite remember and never quite forget.

"Love triumphs! Love delights!
The love of the Sacred Heart rejoices!"

As Margaret looked up in wonder, the angels spoke to her: "Sing, sing with us, our sister! Sing the praises of this Divine Heart!"

"I dare not sing with you!"

"But you must sing, for we have come to join with you in paying a continual homage of love, of adoration, of praise! And for this reason we will always take your place before the Blessed Sacrament, so that even when you are not there, you can love without ceasing! And you, in your turn, must take our place on earth!"

"But how can I take your places, you blessed ones!"

"By suffering for us, since we ourselves cannot suffer! By sharing in your suffering, we share in your love. You must rejoice, by means of us, and we will suffer by means of you!"

Thus the saint became an associate of the celestial Seraphim, whose fiery love her own love so much resembled. And thus all the sufferings of her life were sanctified anew, as human suffering has rarely been sanctified. The vision lasted for nearly two hours. But the haunting memory of it lasted until the day on which she greeted her angelic associates face to face.

EIGHT • THE TRIUMPH OF THE SACRED HEART

Mother Greyfié's term of office ended in 1684. Mother Marie-Christine Melin, who had been a nun in the Paray monastery for thirty-four years, was chosen to succeed her. The new superior's outstanding virtue was her great sweetness of character. She was kind and gentle and had a great reputation as a peacemaker in the community.

This made one of Mother Melin's first acts as superior doubly surprising to many of the nuns. She named Sister Alacoque as her first and strong choice for assistant superior. And assistant superior Sister Alacoque was promptly elected. No one in the convent was more distressed by this turn of events than Sister Alacoque herself. It was a new kind of sacrifice for her. She found it much harder to bear than any of the trials and humiliations that Mother Greyfié had handed out so freely.

Margaret's unexpected new authority was useful to her in at least one way. When she was assigning the household chores, she always gave herself the lowliest ones she could find, like washing up the pots and pans for the lay sisters. One day, while she was sweeping out the chapel, she was called away to settle a problem that had arisen in the kitchen. From there she was called to another job. A few hours later, as she hurried into the chapel at the sound of the office bell, she was greeted by a dreadful sight. The entire community was filing into the choir past one large pile of dust, one broom, and one dustpan that the assistant superior had left, completely forgotten in the middle of the floor.

In December of that year the mistress of novices became ill and had to retire. One of th most important positions in the convent had to be filled at once. A really good mistress of novices needs a natural talent that is rarely found. While Mother Melin sat in her office one day, thinking over the problem, she heard a timid knock at the door. The four novices of the community stood outside. They had come to ask a great favor of their superior, they explained. Could they please have Sister Alacoque for their new mother?

The superior looked into the eager young faces and smiled. "Well, my dears," she said, "and why do you want Sister Alacoque for your mistress?"

The girls looked hopefully at one another, each one waiting for somebody else to say something. Finally the youngest one blurted out, "Because we know that Sister Alacoque can make us holy in spite of ourselves!"

And that is exactly what happened. Love is contagious, so naturally the novices began to imitate the fervor of their new mother. Soon the spirit that radiated from the novitiate became so exciting that two of the young nuns, professed a short time before, asked for permission to go back to the novitiate to spend a few months under Sister Alacoque's direction.

In the novitiate, for the first time, Margaret was able to talk, freely and without fear, about

the subject closest to her heart. To her novices
who loved her and trusted her in everything, she
unfolded the rich treasures of the Sacred Heart,
just as Claude de la Colombière had revealed
them to the Jesuit seminarians. Ideas that seem
new and different do not flourish unless they are
entrusted to young people, who are not afraid to
think new thoughts. The little novices quickly
caught the fire of their mistress.

So did some of the professed sisters. Sister
Marie Rosalie and several of her friends used to
slip discreetly off to the novitiate whenever they
could, to hear Margaret talk to her novices about
the great love of the Sacred Heart, a love that
struck an answering chord in their own generous hearts. Among them was Sister Dusson, the
lay sister who ran the kitchen so efficiently and
who grew and sold the most profitable vegetables
in convent history. Everybody loved Sister Dusson for her sharp wit and warm heart. And Sister
Dusson loved everybody back, but most of all
she loved Sister Alacoque.

For the first time since the death of Père
Claude, Margaret had the joy of sharing the great
feast that they had once kept together. On the
Friday after the octave of Corpus Christi, while
the rest of the community followed its usual
weekday schedule, the novitiate quietly celebrated

the feast of the Sacred Heart with special prayers before the Blessed Sacrament.

Shortly afterwards, on the twentieth of July, came the feast of St. Margaret. For a week before, the novices had been plotting surprises and presents for their beloved mother on her feast day. She noticed that at her approach whispered conversations were hushed up and bits of colored paper and ribbon disappeared up the nearest sleeve. The day before the feast she said to the girls, "My dears, I know very well what you are up to, and I would like to ask a great favor of you. May I tell you in advance what I would like to have for my feast day?"

The girls agreed eagerly.

"My feast day falls on a Friday," Margaret went on. "Let us dedicate the day together to the Sacred Heart of Jesus. Let us reserve for Him whatever surprises and honors you were planning for me. Is it agreed?"

The novices were delighted, for this gave them a great new opportunity for plotting. The minute Margaret was out of sight they put their heads together and began to buzz.

The next day a greatly irritated Sister des Escures was knocking at the superior's door. "*Ma mère*, although I dislike doing so, I must complain to you about the novices!"

"Yes, Sister?" said Mother Melin, looking up from her work.

"I can hardly bring myself to believe such a thing. But I am sure that the novices were out of their beds last night. At midnight! I distinctly heard footsteps on the novitiate stairway. And then noise in the refectory. And *then*—" She lowered her voice as though she could hardly bear to say the rest—"I heard giggling!"

Mother Melin cleared her throat hastily to avoid doing something along those lines herself. "You are quite right, Sister. It *was* the novices. Since you say they giggled and made noise, I promise to scold them at once."

"B-but—may I ask—what were the novices doing up at midnight?"

"They were cleaning the refectory."

"At *midnight*?"

"Yes. They asked permission to do their chores during the night, since they have something very important to do today." She smiled. "Think, Sister. What day is today?"

Sister des Escures thought. "Oh yes. It is the feast of St. Margaret." She sighed. "Heaven only knows *what* those novices are up to today!"

When Margaret went into the novices' community room the next morning, she saw exactly what the novices had been up to. They had begged and borrowed a cloth, some candles and flowers. With the aid of two chairs and a plank, they had built a little altar. Pinned to the cloth was a simple pen and ink drawing that they had made of the Heart of Christ. It was the first altar to the Sacred Heart that Margaret had ever seen. Barely able to hold back her tears, she knelt before it with her novices. Together they recited the prayer of consecration that she had written.

It was a small beginning—small as a mustard seed.

The enthusiasm of the novices was so great that they made one mistake. "If only the whole community could see our lovely altar!" said one of the girls toward evening.

"Oh, yes! Dear Mother, *please* let us invite them to come and see it. *Please!*"

Margaret hesitated. She knew it was not a very good idea, but the eagerness of the girls was too much for her. "Well—why not? Go and invite them. Sister Françoise-Rosalie, you go—"

Little Sister Verchère hurried down to the main part of the convent. She tried to walk at a dignified pace, although she was bursting with excitement. As luck would have it, the first person she met was Sister des Escures, who was walking with a group of the older nuns. Sister Verchère politely issued her invitation. The

novices had made an altar in honor of the Sacred
Heart of Jesus, to honor their mistress's feast day.
Would the sisters do them the great favor of
coming to the novitiate to visit their altar?

There was a moment of shocked silence. Auto-
matically the other nuns looked toward Sister
des Escures.

"My *dear* child," she said sternly, drawing herself up to her full, impressive height, "will you
please go back to the novitiate and tell your mistress that it is not for her and for you novices to
establish new devotions in this community—as
she would soon find out by reading Constitution
Number Eighteen! She will be doing quite enough
if she teaches you to practice the rule correctly.
It is *not* necessary to change all of you into—
into—*visionaries* like herself!"

Even as she spoke Sister des Escures knew that
she was being unkind, but she could not help
herself. Teaching new, unapproved devotions to
novices! What an idea! She went off down the
hall in a terrible humor, muttering Constitution
Number Eighteen to herself.

Poor Sister Verchère went back to the novitiate
feeling as though someone had just emptied a
pail of cold water over her. The other girls
greeted her at the door, all talking at once. "What

did they say?" "When are they coming?" "How many of them did you see?"

Sister Verchère looked into the happy faces and gulped. "Uh—they said they couldn't come today," she hedged, not daring to look Sister Alacoque in the eye.

Margaret smiled sadly. "What you mean is that they *won't* come. But leave them alone. They will change their minds. The Sacred Heart will make them. But He wants everything by love and nothing by force. We must wait—"

It did not take long for the story of St. Margaret's day to reach the ears of the superior. Peace-loving Mother Melin, who liked to make everybody happy, was greatly distressed. "Oh dear," she thought, "if only those silly little girls had kept this to themselves and not spread it all over the convent—! Now that everyone knows about it, I shall have to take a stand. Sister des Escures is perfectly right. There *is* Constitution Number Eighteen!"

She summoned the mistress of novices and announced her decision. No more altars to the Sacred Heart! No more devotions to the Sacred Heart! No more *talk* about the Sacred Heart! But the look on Margaret's face was too much for her own kind heart. "Of course, Sister," she added quickly, "if you wish to continue some little of this devotion of yours in the privacy of the novitiate—well, you *are* the mistress of novices. But as far as the rest of the community is concerned, this devotion to the Sacred Heart simply does not exist!"

This was a cruel blow for Margaret and her novices. Not only were they exactly where they had started from, but they had exposed their beloved devotion to ridicule and ill-will on the part of the other nuns. "I feared nothing so much as that this Divine Heart might be dishonored," Margaret wrote. "Everything that was said to me was like a sword piercing my heart."

"But don't be afraid!" the familiar voice told her. *"I will reign in spite of all those who oppose Me!"*

"Then I will give You the task of defending Your own cause," Margaret told Him, smiling in the middle of her tears. "And from now on I will simply suffer in silence."

Defend Your own cause!

The Lord waited for the proper moment and then proceeded to follow her instructions. There was only one logical choice of "lawyer" to take over this cause of His. Someone had already been chosen for that purpose. To defend the cause in its present crisis, the Lord chose His faithful servant and friend, Claude de la Colombière.

Nearly four and a half years had passed since the death of Père Claude, but he had not been forgotten in Paray-le-Monial. A great devotion to the would-be martyr had sprung up among the people of the town. There was no doubt in anyone's mind that he would one day be officially venerated by the Church.

To understand what happened next, we must keep in mind the fact that at the present moment only two people in the world knew all about the great revelations that Margaret had once confided to the Jesuit: Margaret herself and Mother Saumaise.

After Père Claude's death, his superiors had discovered his diaries and papers lying among his few poor possessions. To leave these spiritual treasures buried in the archives, they realized, would be a terrible loss to the world. The strong and beautiful writings of the dead priest were edited and published under the title *Spiritual Retreat*. In due time a copy of this book reached the Visitation nuns of Paray-le-Monial.

For months Mother Melin had been searching her soul in the matter of Sister Alacoque and her beloved devotion to the Sacred Heart. As she read through the inspired pages of Father de la Colombière she found herself wishing that he were still alive to help her solve the dilemma.

She sighed and then turned the page. Suddenly she felt as though the words she was reading at that moment had lit up before her eyes like a thousand candles. She could hardly believe what she saw. She reread the page several times and then closed the book.

When her assistant came in for the day's instructions, the superior handed her the volume. "Would you please ask Sister Dusson to put this book on the reader's stand? It will be our reading in the refectory for this week." She smiled and added, "I think the sisters will find it most illuminating."

The refectory was unusually hot on that August day. Margaret was seldom without a splitting headache these days since a dreadful accident she had recently had with a heavy pump handle. The strain of having to eat when she could hardly hold up her head was a cruel one. But she tried to keep her mind on the reading of the new book, for it was sweet to hear the words of her beloved friend in the Sacred Heart.

Suddenly, to her horror, she heard the reader say: "Concluding this retreat, full of confidence in the mercy of my God, I vowed to secure by all possible means the execution of what was ordered by my adorable Master, by procuring the accomplishment of His desires *concerning the devotion which He had suggested to a person to whom He imparts Himself most intimately. . . .*"

Margaret had a strong and terrible premonition of what was coming. She closed her eyes and hoped, as she had never before in her life, for a sudden death.

"God then having disclosed Himself to the person whom one has reasons to believe to be close to His Heart, by the great graces which He has accorded to her, she opened herself to me about it and I obliged her to put in writing what she had told me. . . ."

The reader that day was one of Margaret's former novices and strongest supporters. She faltered over these words for a fraction of a second, and then read on in a loud, clear voice. " 'Being,' said this holy soul, 'before the Blessed Sacrament, one day during Its octave, I received from my God excessive graces of His love. . . .' "

A description of Margaret's last great vision followed. "Behold this Heart Which has so loved mankind . . . !" It was all there, exactly as she had told him. But neither she nor he would ever have dreamed that it would one day be the reading material in the refectory at Paray-le-Monial!

The rule of keeping one's eyes lowered in the refectory was broken by many eyes that day.

Sister de Farges, Margaret's most devoted novice, looked straight at her former mistress and saw a look of such utter misery on her face that she had to use all her self-control not to rush over and console her.

The bell rang. The reading stopped. Silence in the room was customary, but today the silence was almost unbearable. In the hearts of many of the good nuns, who had only been trying to follow the rule and do what was expected of them, great questions arose. All this nonsense with the novices—all this talk about the Sacred Heart—had Claude de la Colombière, the saint and scholar, really known about all this years before his death? Had he believed it? Had all those long, irritating consultations with Sister Alacoque in the parlor been about this? And while Sister Alacoque in Paray-le-Monial had kept silence for so many years, had he, the great preacher, the confidant of kings, really been spreading this devotion of hers in England?

Young Sister de Farges was a good nun, but she had a very human, healthy reaction to what had happened. She was simply delighted with it. At recreation she marched straight up to Margaret and said, "Well, Sister, you certainly had things your way today! Father de la Colombière couldn't have identified you more obviously if he had written your name!''

Margaret looked at her with troubled eyes. "I have just cause to love my abasement," she said, and hurried away to the garden to escape the glances of curious eyes.

Père de la Colombière's book reached other Visitation convents in France. In Semur, some ninety miles away, Mother Greyfié had read it too, even before the reading in the Paray refectory. She looked back across the years and remembered that she had once told a shy young nun, "I want you to forget all these things you are saying about establishing devotion to the Sacred Heart. Put it out of your mind!"

Mother Greyfié was still a woman of action. When she changed her mind, she changed it all the way. She summoned an artist whom she knew and had a long private consultation with him.

Some months later a package arrived at Paray-le-Monial addressed to Sister Alacoque. "From Semur," said Sister Marie Rosalie de Lyonne, who was handing out the mail that day.

"Yes—this is Mère Greyfié's handwriting," said Margaret. "She must be sending us some books for the novices, or—" She had pulled open the wrapping paper and was now looking into the package, unable to say another word.

Sister de Lyonne looked too and then gasped
in admiration. "Oh, Sister!" she said. "How beautiful!" Inside the package was a beautiful miniature painting of the Sacred Heart. "And look!"
Marie Rosalie exclaimed, "She has sent twelve
little copies of it as well! There's a letter, too,
Sister. Do read it!"

Margaret's hands were trembling. But she man-
aged to open the letter and read it aloud. Mother
Greyfié told her that the whole community at
Semur had consecrated itself to the Sacred Heart.
She had ordered the original painting for her own
convent, but it had seemed only fair to her that
Sister Alacoque and her friends should have a
miniature of it and some smaller copies besides.
In this way each novice and each of the professed
sisters who wished to have a picture of the Sacred
Heart could now have one.

"Oh, Sister!" said Marie Rosalie, gathering up
the small pictures. "Let's take them to the novit-
ate at once and—" She stopped abruptly, then
said, "Good morning, *ma soeur*. I didn't see you."

Sister Madeleine des Escures, however, had
been there for some time. She looked at the painting in Margaret's hand and said simply, "Mother
Greyfié sent you this?"

Margaret nodded silently.

Sister des Escures turned and left the community room. She went to chapel and stayed there for some time, having quite a conversation with herself.

"Sister Alacoque!" said Sister des Escures, stopping Margaret on her way to the garden. Some months had passed. It was June again, and the Octave of Corpus Christi was drawing to a close.

Margaret was on her way to gather some flowers for the little altar with which she and the novices planned a quiet celebration of their private feast day. "Good morning, *ma soeur*," said Margaret brightening. Strange as it seemed, the two had become friends, in spite of their great differences of opinion about how to observe the rule.

The older nun said hastily, "Uh—Sister—that little picture that Mother Greyfié sent you—where is it?"

Margaret reached into her pocket and pulled out the miniature. "Why, here it is, Sister."

"I would like to borrow it for a little while —for a day or two. To show it to some of the other sisters," she added hastily.

Margaret had planned to use the miniature on the novices' altar. But no matter, she thought. They could use one of the small copies. "Cer-

tainly, Sister," she said, handing over the picture
and trying to figure out the peculiar expression
on her friend's face.

Sister des Escures took the picture and went
off without another word. Margaret went on to
the garden. On her way she met her dear Sister
Dusson carrying an armful of beautiful roses
from her carefully tended bushes. "Good morning, Sister," Margaret said. "What marvelous
roses! Are they for Benediction tonight?"

At the sound of Margaret's voice, Sister Dusson looked up with a start, as though she had just
been caught stealing apples from the kitchen garden. Then she smiled weakly and rushed into the
building.

Something, Margaret thought, is going on.

The next day was Friday, the twenty-first of
June, 1686.

Eleven years had now passed since Our Lord
has asked that the Friday after the octave of
Corpus Christi be set aside as a feast dedicated to
His Sacred Heart. As long as she lived, Margaret
thought, on her way to the chapel that morning,
she herself would keep the sacred feast. But what
a small response this seemed to a direct request
from heaven.

Margaret entered the choir and genuflected
before the grille. She started to take her place,

then stopped and looked again at the unbelievable sight that greeted her eyes as they became accustomed to the dim light.

There was a chair before the grille, covered with a beautiful piece of cloth. The chair was surrounded by flowers—Sister Dusson's prize roses. And in the center of it was the miniature of the Sacred Heart, resting in a beautiful gold frame.

As Margaret moved nearer to the lovingly-made altar, she saw that a scroll was attached to it. It was an invitation "to all the brides of the Lord to come and pay honor to His Adorable Heart." There was no possibility of mistaking the handwriting on this invitation. No one in the convent wrote as elegant and powerful a hand as Sister Madeleine des Escures.

Margaret turned and found herself looking into the smiling face of Mother Melin. Sister des Escures was behind her, and then, in order of their rank, the rest of the community, waiting to kneel before the new altar of the Sacred Heart.

Seventy-nine years would pass before the great feast day was approved by the Holy See, and ninety-one more years would pass before it was officially extended to the entire Church by Pope Pius IX. Those who loved the Sacred Heart of Jesus fought an uphill struggle during those years.

They fought with the Jansenists, those men of cold hearts. They fought with the Rationalists, those men of cold reason. They fought with theologians and politicians. Their work was interrupted by wars and revolutions. But of all the triumphant battles that the Sacred Heart was to win in later years, none was greater than the battle it had won that summer day in the Visitation chapel of Paray-le-Monial.

NINE • THE HEIRESS TO THE TREASURE

"We will build a chapel," said Mother Melin that afternoon at recreation. "A chapel in honor of the Sacred Heart, right here in the garden! Of course, I don't know where the money will come from. But we'll build a chapel!"

Sister Dusson turned and looked critically in the direction of her kitchen garden. "I know where *some* of the money will come from, *ma mère*!" she said firmly. "From my vegetables!"

"But Sister dear, you already make as much money as you can possibly make from your vegetables!"

"But Mother," said the gardener, with a far-away look in her eyes, "next year they're going to grow twice as big!"

And they did. Whether by prayer or by compost or by a combination of the two, Sister Dusson's garden became a positive gold mine the next spring. Other money began to come in from other unexpected sources. The Sisters of the Little Habit got together and voted their entire stock of candy money for the chapel. Relatives of the nuns sent gifts. As word spread around the town, friends of the relatives, and friends of the friends, and, finally, total strangers began to send great and small contributions. Much sooner than anyone had hoped for, the workmen were called in to start digging the foundation.

Toward the end of the year 1868, Margaret's term as novice mistress ended. Several of her novices, now professed, "graduated" from the novitiate at the same time. With them they brought their most prized possession: the miniature of the Sacred Heart that Mother Greyfié had sent them.

In the novitiate, the miniature had occupied a place of honor in the novices' community room.

But where could they put it in the main part of the building?

Mother Melin thought over their problem for a moment and said, "Do you know that little broom closet under the back stairway? Well, surely we can find someplace else to keep the brooms."

Once the young sisters had permission, they made the switch from closet to oratory in record time. When it had been scrubbed and white-washed, they painted the walls with a wonderful, simple-hearted array of flowers, fruits and stars.

"Of course, it's very lovely," Sister des Escures announced one day, when the little room was finished. "But it will simply *not* stay in order unless one person makes it her responsibility to *keep* it in order!"

"Oh, you're right, Sister dear," said Sister Verchère. "But I wonder whom we could ask to be our sacristan. Let's see—perhaps Sister Anne Rosselin, or—"

"*I*," said Sister des Escures firmly, "will be the sacristan!"

No chapel, church, or cathedral in the world was ever tended so lovingly and jealously as the little closet under the stairs was cared for by Sister Madeleine des Escures, "the living rule." She dusted it, swept it, and polished it until, as

Margaret wrote later, "It is a little jewel, so well does she care for it." In her own stately hand the sacristan copied out little books of prayers to the Sacred Heart, for the use of those who came to pray. These books became so popular that they kept disappearing. Finally Sister des Escures wrote sternly on each one, "Will you please have the goodness *not* to take this away!" And after that nobody dared to do it.

The devotion began to spread rapidly, as fire always spreads over parched and dry earth. In the Visitation convent at Dijon, where Mother Saumaise now lived, a little sister named Jeanne-Madeleine Joly wrote the first book of devotions to the Sacred Heart and composed a Mass for the feast day. Margaret herself wrote to the Visitation nuns in Moulins about the devotion. In doing so she proved herself truly a lawyer's daughter. She wrote, straight-faced: "We found this devotion in the book of the *Retreat* by the Reverend Father de la Colombière whom people venerate as a saint." And this was the absolute truth. They *had* "found the devotion" there.

It was a source of great joy to Margaret that two of the earliest apostles of the Sacred Heart outside of the convent were her two brothers, Jacques and Chrysostome. One was the parish priest of Bois-Sainte-Marie and the other was mayor of the village. Between them they built a chapel to the Sacred Heart and announced to the population that as of immediately everyone would kindly attend Solemn Mass on the first Friday of each month.

As the word spread, a new kind of trial came to plague Margaret. She herself became an object of great interest and devotion. She had already gone through a cruel ordeal when her confessor, Father Rolin, S.J., had ordered her to write the story of her life. Now other priests were calling at the convent, asking to see her. Often they had good reasons for doing so. More and more pamphlets and books about the Sacred Heart were being published. Their authors naturally wanted to check the facts with the only living expert on the subject, but there was nothing Margaret dreaded more than having to visit with someone face to face in the parlor.

It was sometime during this last period of the saint's life that God revealed to her still another reward for those who revere the Sacred Heart of Jesus. He would grant the gift of final repentance, of death in the state of grace, to all those who receive Communion on the first Friday of the month, for nine successive months. Thus began one of the most widespread of all devotions to the Sacred Heart.

On September 7, 1688, the little chapel in the northeast corner of the garden was dedicated. Mother Saumaise had sent a beautiful painting of the Sacred Heart to hang in the little building.

The entire population of Paray-le-Monial joined in the celebration. By noon the townspeople, accompanied by hundreds of pilgrims from the neighboring country parishes, were patiently lined up outside the gates, and were finally admitted to the garden.

Most of the people who came to see the chapel dedicated were hoping for a word with, or at least a glimpse of, Sister Alacoque. But they were disappointed. Margaret, kneeling inside the chapel, was caught up in an ecstasy of pure happiness and love the moment Benediction began. She did not awaken from this heavenly dream until long after the gate had closed behind the last pilgrim.

The pride which the residents of Paray-le-Monial take in the Sacred Heart chapel has lasted for almost three centuries. On every feast of the Sacred Heart the gates of that carefully cloistered garden are again opened to the townspeople, now joined by pilgrims from all over the world, who come on that day to pay homage to the Sacred Heart of Jesus and to their own special saint, who lies buried only a few hundred feet from the main road of the town.

It was time for the sisters to make their annual retreats, or "solitudes." "It is my turn to go into solitude now," Margaret said one day to Sister Marest. "But it will be the great solitude!" She knew that her death was near because her sufferings were over, and with them, her reason for living.

On the eve of her retreat she was seized by a sudden fever and quickly put to bed. Dr. Billet, who had brought her through much more serious illnesses, was not alarmed. "You'll soon be up and around, Sister!" he told her. "I'd even make a wager on it!"

But Margaret knew that she was dying and in her last hours of life one fear haunted her: the thought that she would be remembered and revered after death. She called her former novice, Sister de Farges, to her bedside and said in a whisper, "Dear Sister, you must do me one last service! Take this key and go to my top bureau drawer. There you will see a notebook, written in my handwriting. It is the story of my life that I wrote under the orders of my confessor. Find it and burn it! *Please*, dear Sister! Go quickly!"

Fortunately for us, Sister Alacoque had picked the wrong messenger for such an errand. Nothing in the world would have persuaded the young nun to burn that notebook. But she hated to re-

fuse anything to her dying friend, and she was
unwilling to lie to her. She thought quickly.
"Listen, Sister dear—give me the key, yes, but
let me give it to our superior. Let *her* decide what
to do with that notebook!" Margaret shook her
head weakly but before she could say anything
the sister added, "Just think! Here is a chance to
make one great sacrifice to God. Perhaps it is the
greatest you have ever made for Him in your
whole life! Can you resist such an opportunity?"

Margaret could not. "She consented to this,
although it cost her a great deal!"

On the evening of October 17, 1690, Margaret asked to be brought the Holy Viaticum.
But the doctor and the other nuns were still convinced that the illness was slight, and she was not
allowed to receive it. Later that night she sent
for the superior and this time asked to be anointed.
"It is time," she said calmly. The superior, looking into the fever-bright eyes of the sick woman,
realized the truth. Sister Alacoque was indeed
dying, although no one but herself had guessed
it. She immediately sent for the priest. "And I
will have the doctor here too, my dear Sister, in
five minutes!"

Margaret smiled feebly. "*Ma mère*," she said,
"I don't need the doctor. I need nothing but God.

I need only to hide myself in the Heart of Jesus Christ."

The priest arrived and quickly began the prayers of Extreme Unction. When he was about halfway through them, Sister Alacoque died, quietly murmuring one word, "Jesus!"

Our Lord had once told St. Margaret Mary that He would make her the heiress of all the treasures of His Sacred Heart, the treasures that she had revealed anew to the world. As her two beloved novices, in whose arms she had died, gently lowered her frail body onto the pillow, her radiant soul, borne on the wings of the flaming Seraphim, sped like a golden arrow to claim its inheritance.

VISION BOOKS